W9-CSB-407

FACTS AT YOUR FINGERTIPS

ENDANGERED ANIMALS

REPTILES AND AMPHIBIANS

Published by Brown Bear Books Limited

4877 N. Circulo Bujia
Tucson, AZ 85718
USA

and

First Floor
9-17 St. Albans Place
London N1 ONX
UK

Library of Congress Cataloging-in-Publication Data

Reptiles and amphibians / edited by Tim Harris.
p. cm. – (Facts at your fingertips. Endangered animals)
Includes bibliographical references and index.
Summary: "Describes various reptiles and amphibians that are endangered and at risk of becoming extinct. Data Sheet sidebars and maps accompany the text"–Provided by publisher.
ISBN 978-1-936333-36-3 (library binding)
1. Rare reptiles–Juvenile literature. 2. Rare amphibians–Juvenile literature. I. Harris, Tim.
QL644.7.R47 2012
333.95'72–dc22
2010053968

ISBN-13 978-1-936333-36-3

Editorial Director: Lindsey Lowe
Editor: Tim Harris
Creative Director: Jeni Child
Designer: Lynne Lennon
Children's Publisher: Anne O'Daly
Production Director: Alastair Gourlay

Printed in the United States of America

In this book you will see the following key at top left of each entry. The key shows the level of threat faced by each animal, as judged by the International Union for the Conservation of Nature (IUCN).

EX	Extinct
EW	Extinct in the Wild
CR	Critically Endangered
EN	Endangered
VU	Vulnerable
NT	Near Threatened
LC	Least Concern
O	Other (this includes Data Deficient and Not Evaluated)

For a few animals that have not been evaluated since 2001, the old status of Lower Risk still applies and this is shown by the letters **LR** on the key.

For more information on Categories of Threat, see pp. 54–57.

Picture Credits

Abbreviations: c=center; t=top; l=left; r=right.

Cover Images
Front: *Hawksbill turtle,* Thinkstock/istockphoto
Back: *Golden toad,* Stocbyte

AL: Edwin Mickleburgh 61; P. Morris 41; **BCC:** Orion Press 39 Pacific Stock 4t; **FLPA:** Frants Hartmann 57, Chris Mattison 43; **IUCN:** 59; **Mark Hutchinson:** 11; **PEP:** Pete Oxford 51; **Photolibrary Group:** Bob Bennett 28–29, Tom Brakefield 49, Marty Cordano 56, Tui De Roy 58, Michael Fogden 22–23, John Gerlach/Animals Animals 8–9, Nick Gordon 27, Daniel Heuclin 4b; Mark Jones 18–19, Paul Kay 12–13, Zig Leszczynski/Animals Animals 17, 20–21, 30–31, 47, Mike Linley 45, Stan Osolinski 54-55, Norbert Rosing 58–59, Mark Webster 15; **Photoshot:** A.N.T 53; **R. Gibson:** 25. **Thinkstock:** Stocbyte 1

CONTENTS

What is a Reptile?

Like all classes of animal, reptiles are divided into groups—crocodilians, lizards, the tuatara, snakes, and chelonians (tortoises and turtles). All reptiles are said to be cold-blooded. More correctly, they are "ectothermic," which means that, unlike mammals and birds, they cannot produce heat inside the body, but rely instead on heat from external sources—mainly sunlight—to raise their body temperatures. When their bodies have warmed up sufficiently, they are able to engage in normal activities such as feeding. The ectothermic reptiles need less food and have colonized deserts (where food is scarce) as well as every other type of habitat, except where the land is permanently frozen.

Birds are covered in feathers, and mammals are covered in hair, but reptiles have a covering of scales, although in some cases the scales are so small and smooth that they resemble skin.

Reptiles have developed numerous shapes, sizes, colors, and other features that enable them to live in their own particular niche. Although some species may be able to adapt to a changed habitat, many depend on a particular habitat and conditions; marine turtles and some freshwater turtles are totally aquatic, leaving the water only to lay eggs. Some aquatic species can only feed in water, although they spend much of their time on land (see yellow-blotched sawback map turtle, pp. 16–17).

Lizards show much more variation in body form than other reptiles; some forms are long and snakelike with no limbs; others may have only two limbs. Among the lizards there are burrowing species that hardly ever come above ground. The speed of movement of reptiles varies; tortoises are generally slow-moving creatures that rely on withdrawing into their shell for protection and are easy to capture. Some lizards are slow moving but capable of a quick burst of speed; others are agile and quick-moving.

Among the snakes and lizards several different lifestyles exist; some are aquatic, others terrestrial or arboreal; and there are also semiaquatic and burrowing forms. Many reptiles hide in disused animal burrows or dig their own. Some shelter under rocks or logs, and others burrow or shuffle into the soil for shelter. Many reptiles are actually beneficial to farmers and gardeners because they eat large

The Senegal chameleon *(below) of West Africa. Chameleons are one of a number of reptiles that have evolved to follow a specialized lifestyle and seldom manage to adapt to changed conditions.*

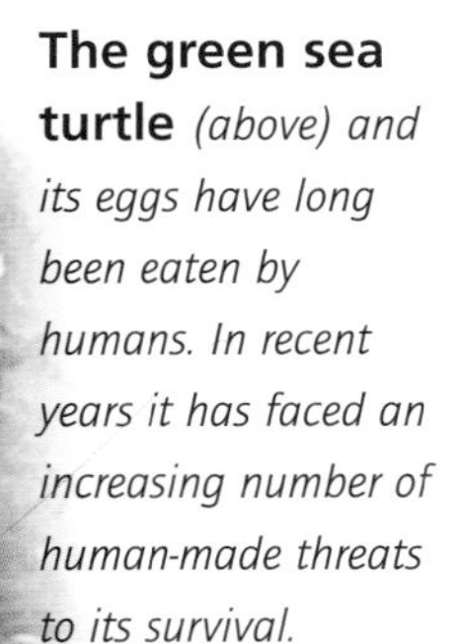

The green sea turtle *(above) and its eggs have long been eaten by humans. In recent years it has faced an increasing number of human-made threats to its survival.*

numbers of insects; others predate rodents, thus keeping numbers down.

The History of Reptiles

The earliest reptiles known from fossilized remains are estimated to have lived 315 million years ago. In the millions of years that followed, a multitude of different forms evolved. Those that survived when the dinosaurs died out gradually developed into the forms we see today. Two reptile groups—the crocodilians and the chelonians—have changed little in 65 million years, apart from now being smaller than their ancestral forms. Since 1600, 21 forms have become extinct, and 454 forms are threatened.

Why are Reptiles at Risk?

The decline of a particular species may be due to a combination of causes, but the greatest single threat to all animals is habitat destruction. The lifestyles and characteristics of reptiles make them vulnerable to many of the human-made threats. Habitat destruction takes numerous forms, such as land clearance, and most reptile species cannot adapt to changed habitat.

Land can be cleared by tree-felling, burning, or large-scale construction machinery. Arboreal reptiles suffer from the loss of trees. For example, chameleons are threatened in many regions by deforestation. They are superb examples of adaptation to arboreal life, with their divided feet and prehensile tails. Only a few species manage to adapt to living in secondary forest, which sometimes grows when farm land has been abandoned. If the land has been turned over to crops or cattle, the original vegetation disappears. Unless there is suitable habitat nearby into which reptiles can move (if they have not been killed during land clearance), they begin to die out.

Although fires can be natural, they are a threat, particularly to slow-moving animals such as desert tortoises and geometric tortoises, but in some cases the creatures may survive by sheltering in burrows (for example, eastern indigo snakes). However, in some areas, notably Madagascar and Indonesia, deliberate burning that can get out of control is causing devastation to plants and animals.

Deforestation leads to soil erosion, especially along river banks, and destroys nesting areas of many freshwater turtles (for example, pig-nosed turtles). In turn, soil erosion leads to the silting up of rivers, necessitating dredging equipment to clear and deepen the water, which disturbs their habitat further. Silt carried out to sea destroys coral reefs where some marine turtles feed. In some countries land along river banks has been cleared for housing, thus bringing the native people into conflict with aquatic reptiles (see gharial, pp. 30–31).

Modern construction equipment can quickly alter large areas of habitat, destroying any creatures that do not move fast enough. Reptiles that are hibernating, estivating, or simply sheltering are vulnerable to land clearance.

Since life appeared *on earth, many animal species have become extinct, like these various types of giant land and sea reptiles. Extinctions are part of the natural process, but the impact of human population increase has accelerated the dangers facing many species.*

Lizards *are probably the most familiar of the reptiles because of their diversity and wide distribution. Examples include the ocellated green lizard (1), fat-tailed gecko (2), western skink (3), blue-tongued skink (4), a sharp-snouted snake Pygopodidae (5), and Colorado checkered whiptail (6).*

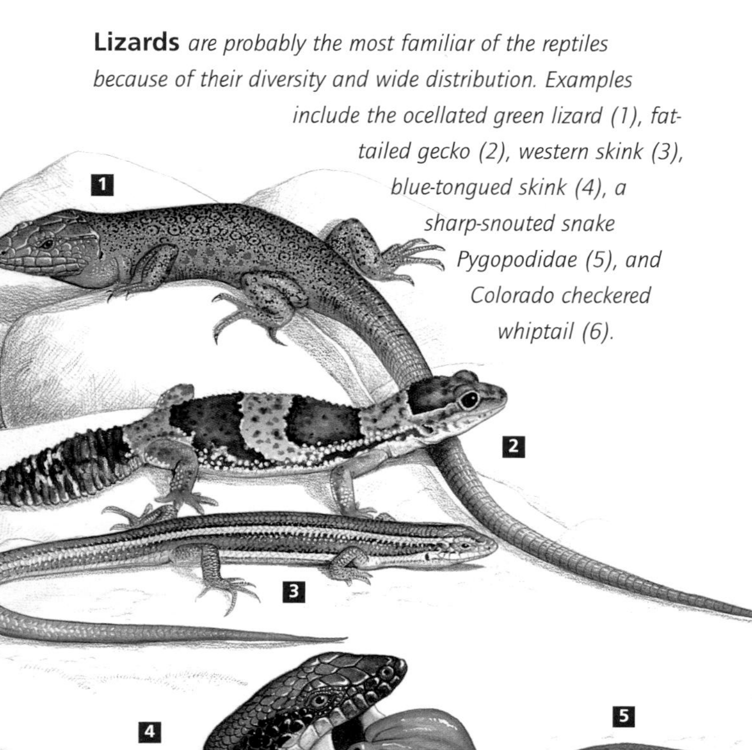

The emerald boa *(above) is threatened by the destruction of tropical rain forest, since it feeds and gives birth in trees. Destruction of habitats also removes huge numbers of insects, which are an important part of the food chain and support other species of reptile, especially lizards.*

Plowing is particularly dangerous to creatures that live in isolated areas of grassland (see pygmy blue-tongued skink, pp. 10–11), and plowing a field could possibly wipe out a whole population of a particular reptile species. In addition, since many reptiles bury their eggs, they are destroyed by such activities. Particularly vulnerable are those species that lay small clutches, since it is more difficult for population numbers to increase (for example, Fijian crested iguanas and leopard snakes). Farming and industry bring additional threats such as chemical pollution and waste products. The effects of pollution are many and varied—spraying insecticides, for example, wipes out the insects on which many lizards rely; it can also directly poison reptiles (see blunt-nosed leopard lizard, pp. 8–9). Turtles need clean, unpolluted water; while some can withstand a degree of certain types of pollution, the danger is that the aquatic creatures on which they feed are wiped out.

Drainage of swamp areas for farming and building forces some species into an ever-decreasing habitat. Habitats have become fragmented in many parts, leaving a few isolated areas that prevent contact between populations (see Jamaican boa, pp. 20–21). That causes inbreeding, which eventually produces weaknesses, deformities, and reduced fertility in future generations, further affecting survival. Leisure activities affect reptiles—many beaches used by marine turtles for thousands of years for nesting have disappeared under development (see hawksbill turtle, pp. 14–15). Reptiles such as snakes and lizards are sometimes killed to avoid frightening tourists. Off-road vehicles cause great damage to the burrows and nests of reptiles (see gila monster, pp. 32–33).

Hunting and Exploitation

Deliberate killing of some reptile species is quite common. Many people believe that all reptiles are venomous, although very few are in fact dangerous to humans. Large reptiles such as alligators and crocodiles can, however, be dangerous to people and can prey on domestic livestock (see Chinese alligator, pp. 26–27, American crocodile, pp. 28–29), so they are often killed. They have also been regarded as "big game" and hunted for sport. In many parts of the world some reptiles feature in the diet of the native people. Where hunting is excessive, it can be a serious threat to the survival of a species (see Galápagos giant tortoise, pp. 18–19). Turtle eggs and some lizard eggs are taken for food, which, combined with other factors, causes endangerment. Exploitation includes the use of reptile skins and shells. Huge numbers of reptiles are used in traditional medicine in various regions; the rarer a creature is, the more its value.

The pet trade is often accused of depleting reptile populations. This may be true in some cases (for example, yellow-blotched sawback map turtle, pp. 16–17), but controls on the trade are continually being tightened. Despite this, smuggling livestock for trade, skins, food, and medicine still occurs in many regions of the world.

Threats to Island Populations

Island populations are highly vulnerable to collection for food (see Galápagos giant tortoise, pp. 18–19), destruction of their habitat (see Milos viper, pp. 24–25), or competition for food (see Komodo dragon, pp. 12–13), and natural disasters. The vegetation of many islands has been eaten by introduced animals such as goats and pigs that escaped and reproduced, with devastating results. Rats, cats, and dogs colonized many islands. Without any natural predators to keep numbers down, they too have taken their toll of reptiles living in restricted island habitats (see Jamaican boa, pp. 20–21).

A crocodile head ashtray. *This and similar grisly souvenirs are hardly essential to humans, but many people are still tempted to buy them. Often they are from an endangered creature and it is illegal to sell or import them in many countries.*

The Situation Today

Extinction of some species is part of a natural process, but it normally takes thousands or even millions of years. Today, with the growth of the human population, extinction has speeded up and will no doubt accelerate further. Although relatively few of the total number of reptile species are listed as Endangered, many face similar threats to those that challenge their Endangered relatives. Certain species, such as the Galápagos land iguana, Galápagos giant tortoise (pp. 18–19), and Komodo dragon (pp. 12–13), stand out more than others, and their plight has made them the focus of well-publicized conservation work.

Conservation attempts will continue, but some species will become extinct because of the pressure on their habitats from expanding human populations. Zoos and other institutions have limited space and funds, and so must limit the creatures they keep. Conservation in the wild is also restricted by funds and needs the support of local people. It is often difficult to convince people that creatures they fear or dislike are worth saving; but attitudes are slowly changing.

EX
EW
CR
EN
VU
NT
LC
O

Blunt-nosed Leopard Lizard

Gambelia sila

The decline of this attractive lizard dates back to the California Gold Rush of 1849, when parts of its habitat were turned over to agriculture to feed the influx of miners.

The habitat of the blunt-nosed leopard lizard is now restricted to a number of scattered areas in the San Joaquin Valley in California. The lizards use the deserted burrows of small mammals for shade, shelter, and hibernation in winter. Although they are diurnal (active during the day), leopard lizards tend to shelter during the hottest part of the day. They are often active at air temperatures of up to 104°F (40°C), when the soil temperature is about 122°F (50°C). From September onward the lizards take to their burrows to spend the colder months in a dormant state. Leopard lizards have predators, which is part of the natural balance; but when the lizards are forced into smaller areas by human disturbance, and their vegetation cover is destroyed, they become more exposed and vulnerable to these predators.

DATA PANEL

Blunt-nosed leopard lizard

Gambelia sila

Family: Iguanidae

World population: Probably more than 1,000 adults

Distribution: San Joaquin Valley, California

Habitat: Arid areas, often alkaline, saline or sandy soils with sparse vegetation, rarely above 2,500 ft (800 m)

Size: Length: up to 13 in (33 cm)

Form: Slender lizard with long, "whippy" tail, blunt nose, and spotted throat; variable pattern of dark spots and light bars on yellow, fawn, gray, or dark- brown background; body color lightens with increased temperatures, so spots become indistinct; mated females and juveniles develop orange spots; males have red coloration in the breeding season

Diet: Mainly insects, other lizards, and small mammals

Breeding: One clutch of 2–6 eggs laid per year

Related endangered species: None

Status: IUCN EN

The Human Threat

As the human population increased in the San Joaquin Valley, so did agriculture and urban development. This inevitably encroached on the habitat of the blunt-nosed leopard lizard. Further damage occurred as industries developed around the extraction of oil and minerals. By 1985 barely 10 percent of the original wild land on the San Joaquin Valley floor had been left undeveloped, and in 2007 the lizard was still thought to be in decline.

The road building and landfill dumping that accompanied development in the valley were also destructive to the lizard's habitat, and the damage to the delicate balance of the desert ecosystem largely ignored. Lizards and their habitats were destroyed under construction machinery; roads and irrigation ditches fragmented the lizard's territory. Pesticides sprayed on crops also had a detrimental effect on much of the wildlife.

Leopard lizards are insectivorous—a large part of their diet includes insects—so their food supply can be drastically reduced, or contaminated, by the drift from crop spraying. Where the land has been adapted for pastoral farming, grazing animals eat the natural vegetation and

trample rodent burrows and lizard egg sites. They also break the soil surface, which can cause soil erosion. The removal of natural vegetation through grazing allows nonnative plants to invade, eliminating the open spaces preferred by the lizard. The threats to the blunt-nosed leopard lizard from continuing habitat destruction were highlighted as far back as 1954, but the species was not listed as endangered by the United States Department of the Interior until 13 years later. It was given state listing in 1971.

The blunt-nosed leopard lizard *is active by day and prefers hot, dry, and sparsely vegetated areas. It can run on its hindlegs to escape predators, which include snakes, birds, and mammals.*

Recovery Plans

The first recovery plan for the species was not prepared until 1980 (revised in 1985). Since then numerous studies have been carried out, including aerial surveys, to determine the amount of suitable territory still existing. Some areas have been purchased as reserves, but lack of funding has prevented this in many areas.

Conservation is a complex business needing comprehensive studies of numerous aspects: ecology, population, feeding habits, breeding, and genetic variability. Although much information has now been gathered, the scattered nature of the remaining lizard sites complicates matters because of environmental variation. It may be a long time before all the necessary knowledge is accumulated.

The blunt-nosed leopard lizard has proved itself to be adaptable, often colonizing sites that have been disturbed then abandoned. However, unless the decline of its habitat and its continued isolation in ever-shrinking areas are halted, the species may never recover. Its survival depends on further land acquisition and the construction of "corridors" to allow groups to move between fragmented sites, so preventing the genetic problems that develop in small populations. Its habitat must be protected, improved, and managed in such a way that the land is only used in a manner compatible with the lizard's existence. This is a tall order given the conflicting interests over land use. Recovery of this species will take a very long time; it remains to be seen if it will be successful.

Pygmy Blue-tongued Skink

Tiliqua adelaidensis

The pygmy blue-tongued skink—once a common lizard—was presumed to be extinct, since there had been no sightings after 1959. In 1992, however, one was found inside the body of a dead snake. Surveys carried out in the surrounding region—the grasslands of South Australia's Mount Lofty Ranges—revealed a dozen small sites containing pygmy blue-tongued skinks.

Although less than half the size of the larger blue-tongued skinks familiar to many reptile keepers, the pygmy blue-tongued skink is otherwise similar in appearance. Its common name comes from the blue tongue displayed by most lizards of the genus *Tiliqua*. However, while the pygmy skink's mouth lining is pinkish-blue, its tongue is actually pink. The dramatic color combination provides a startling effect that deters attackers.

The lizard is found in the Mount Lofty Ranges north of Adelaide in South Australia. Unfortunately, the animal's preferred habitat is also highly suitable for farming. The climate is ideal, and the native grassland can be easily plowed. Pasture improvement—a process of replacing native plant species with agricultural species such as hay grasses and crops like alfalfa and clover—has further altered the plant diversity in favor of nonnative species.

Habitat Destruction

At the time when the lizards are most active—during the warm months—the soil is too hard for them to dig their own burrows. As a result, they often live in empty spider burrows dug by the spiders during the winter and early spring, when the soil is moist and soft. Plowing of the land is likely to be particularly destructive to the skink's survival, depriving them of shelter and leaving them exposed to snakes, birds, and other predators.

Before Europeans settled in South Australia, much of the area was native grassland supporting other reptile species, as well as birds and plants. Now only about 2 percent of the original grassland is left. All pygmy blue-tongued sites are found in the few unplowed areas. The undisturbed patches also support rare orchids and other plants, butterflies, and an endangered bird: the plains wanderer. Conserving the remaining grasslands will benefit the pygmy blue-tongues as well as the other rare fauna and flora.

Conservation Projects

The discovery of an extinct species was exciting, and various government bodies, museums, zoos, and universities cooperated in the search for new habitat sites. A recovery plan was devised; its first task was to study skinks in the wild and in captivity.

DATA PANEL

Pygmy blue-tongued skink

Tiliqua adelaidensis

Family: Scincidae (subfamily Lygosominae)

World population: About 5,500

Distribution: North Mount Lofty Ranges, southern South Australia

Habitat: Grassland with tussocks and open areas; open woodland

Size: Length: 7 in (18 cm); males often slightly smaller than females

Form: Heavy body with relatively short limbs; scales small and smooth. Male has larger head than female. Color varies from gray-brown to orange-brown with darker flecks along back

Diet: Insects and some plant material

Breeding: Gives birth to 1–4 live young per year

Related endangered species: No close relatives, but more than 40 other skink species are listed by IUCN

Status: IUCN EN

The pygmy blue-tongued skink *has a heavy body with relatively short limbs and a fairly short tail, and its scales are small and smooth. Despite its name, the skink's tongue is, in fact, mainly pink.*

A group of pygmy blue-tongued skinks was taken to Adelaide Zoo to be studied. Specimens were also displayed to increase public awareness of the lizard's plight. After seven years in captivity the colony had not bred. It was decided to set up another group in private, free from disturbance by the public. Little was known about the animal's behavior and requirements, but captive breeding for possible release into the wild was an important part of the recovery plan.

Pygmy blue-tongues are listed under the Endangered Species Protection Act and the South Australia National Parks and Wildlife Act. An important task has been to persuade landowners to protect known skink habitat sites on their land. There are also several laws that could be enforced to prevent habitat destruction. Law enforcement is perhaps the most important task, since the habitat is fragile and small in area. Some owners of land enclosing sites with good habitat for the species have signed agreements to run their properties as wildlife sanctuaries. Other landowners have been eager to sign up, though there have been legal problems over grazing rights. Two previously unknown sites have also been discovered.

By early 2000 the situation for the pygmy blue-tongued skink had improved. An area of native grassland—unpopulated by the species but close to its other habitats—was made into a conservation park in the hope that it will be suitable for translocations. The park could be the first secure home for the animals.

The total number of blue-tongues is difficult to estimate because of their patchy distribution, but it may be about 5,500. However, the figure is still too low to justify changing the lizard's Endangered status to Vulnerable. Although relatively few populations are unprotected now, the lizard will keep its status until larger populations exist in secure habitats.

One project to increase numbers involves the provision of artificial burrows. They are made from wooden tubes that are the same length and diameter as the favored spider hole, but less easily destroyed. Advising landowners on habitat management, such as weed clearance, grazing, and the use of pesticides, is also an important part of the program. Community involvement is a high priority, and a local school has been involved in studies as part of the plan. Despite such efforts, the outlook for the pygmy blue-tongued skink is by no means certain, since funds for wildlife conservation are limited.

EX
EW
CR
EN
VU
NT
LC
O

Komodo Dragon

Varanus komodoensis

Known locally as buaja daret ("land crocodiles"), these giant lizards were named after the mythical dragon because of their size and fierce predatory nature.

It seems inconceivable that the enormous Komodo dragon could remain unknown (at least to western scientists) until the early 20th century. Referred to locally as the ora or buaja daret ("land crocodile"), early reported sightings were probably dismissed as superstition or simply as crocodiles. In 1912 a Dutch pilot, having swum ashore to the island of Komodo after crashing in the sea, reported seeing them; further investigation verified their existence. The first scientific description was by Major P. A. Ouwens, director of the botanical gardens in Buitenzorg, Java, in 1912. Soon afterward a government order closed the area in which they were found and limited the number of specimens allowed to go to zoos.

The Komodo dragon is found only on Komodo and the neighboring islands of Rinca, Padar, and western Flores. Some of the populations are probably transient—they are powerful swimmers and go from island to island in search of food. The total area of their natural habitat is roughly 390 square miles (1,000 sq. km), and it is generally hot, with an average daytime temperature of 80°F (27°C) or higher. Usually conditions are very dry, too, apart from a short monsoon season, when the Komodo dragons use pools caused by rain for wallowing. During hot weather and overnight they take to burrows.

Komodo dragons are top predators in their range. Adults will tackle anything, including deer, pigs, and goats. Occasionally even humans are said to feature in the diet. They are armed with a strong tail as well as powerful limbs and claws. Their teeth are serrated like those of sharks and can easily rip a carcass. They also produce bacteria that cause blood poisoning and death. Prey that is not killed immediately often dies later. Komodo dragons can scent the carrion up to

DATA PANEL

Komodo dragon

Varanus komodoensis

Family: Varanidae

World population: 4,000–5,500 in the wild

Distribution: Indonesia; islands of Komodo, Rinca, Padar, and western Flores

Habitat: Lowland islands, arid forest, and savanna

Size: Length: males over 8 ft (2.4 m); females 7 ft (2.1 m). Weight: males 200 lb (90 kg); females 150 lb (67 kg)

Form: Lizard with large, bulky body and powerful tail, strong limbs, and claws. Rough scales give a beaded appearance. External ear openings are visible on each side of the head. Sharp teeth for ripping carcasses. Coloration is brown, black, reddish brown, or gray

Diet: Hatchlings and juveniles eat insects, reptiles, eggs, small rodents, and birds. Adults eat deer, pigs, goats, possibly water buffalo, and reputedly, humans

Breeding: Up to 30 eggs, buried. Incubation period about 8 months

Related endangered species: Gray's monitor lizard (*Varanus olivaceus*) VU

Status: IUCN VU

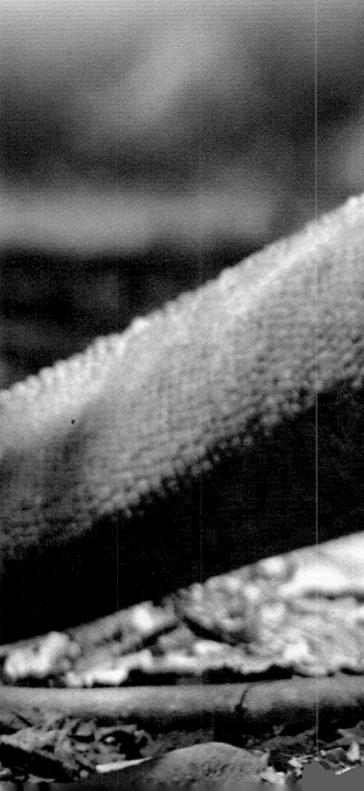

5 miles (8 km) away and come to gather at the site of the death.

The Indonesian government regards Komodo dragons as a national asset, and they are protected. Hunting is strictly forbidden; trade in Komodos (or their parts) is banned under CITES (see p. 60). Tourists on Komodo are carefully controlled to prevent disturbance. The islands of Padar and Rinca are nature reserves where no tourists are allowed. However, Komodo dragons have been smuggled. In 1998 a Malaysian was arrested in Mexico City after investigation by the United States Fish and Wildlife Service, and Komodo dragons were seized.

Protecting the Species

The main threat to Komodo dragons comes from habitat destruction and the poaching of their prey by inhabitants on Komodo Island. Padar and Rinca are uninhabited, so this is not a problem; however, there, as on Komodo, natural fires destroy the plants and animals on which the dragons depend. There have been reports claiming that many specimens on Komodo are emaciated from lack of food.

The first captive-breeding attempt was carried out in the National Zoo, Washington, in 1992, when 13 out of a clutch of 26 eggs hatched; this was followed by two successful hatchings at Cincinnati Zoo in 1993. Currently around 300 specimens are held in zoos worldwide; 186 of the specimens are juveniles bred in captivity. This is encouraging, but many zoos are unable to set up breeding groups due to lack of space. Zoo populations are seen as a "reservoir" from which specimens could be reintroduced into the wild. No further introductions will be made, however, until the genetic makeup of wild and captive-bred specimens has been studied, since variations between the two have been observed.

The Komodo dragon *is a giant lizard about 8 feet (2.4 m) long. The largest recorded example, which was displayed in Saint Louis in the 1930s, measured 10.2 feet (3 m) and weighed over 350 pounds (160 kg).*

EX
EW
CR
EN
VU
NT
LC
O

Hawksbill Turtle

Eretmochelys imbricata

For centuries the hawksbill's attractive shell has been the main source of tortoiseshell. Despite international legislation, illegal trade in this commodity continues, and the hawksbill is one of the most seriously threatened sea turtles in the world.

Sea turtles such as the hawksbill have always been exploited by humans for food, oil, and skins. On a local scale a balance can be maintained, but he pressure of human activities over the last 50 years has resulted in all sea turtle species becoming endangered. Although all species are listed on CITES Appendix I, some of the 150 signatory countries flout the ruling. The hawksbill is classed by the IUCN as Critical, making it one of the most severely endangered sea turtles in the world.

For many years the hawksbill's attractively colored shell has been the main source of tortoiseshell, used for glasses frames, combs, ornaments, and jewelry. The scutes (hornlike shields) of the hawksbill shell are exceptionally thick, making them ideal for carving. Japan has been the largest user, importing an average of 30 tons (305 kg) of shell per year between 1970 and 1994. More than half of this was from the Caribbean—particularly Cuba—and Latin America. In the 1980s Japan's stockpile of hawksbill shell represented the death of over 170,000 turtles.

Although a member of CITES, Japan did not ban shell imports until 1993. Proposals by Cuba to allow the exportation of hawksbill shell to Japan by transferring the species from CITES Appendix I to Appendix II were defeated in 1997 and 2000. However, turtle meat and eggs are still consumed and sold in many countries. Illegal shipments of shell are often intercepted, and tourist souvenirs, including whole turtles, stuffed and lacquered, are openly traded in many countries. Bringing any part of a sea turtle back from vacation is illegal, and seizures, sometimes followed by fines, are common.

Hawksbills have been recorded on the coasts of at least 96 different countries, and nesting takes place only on sandy beaches. Suitable sites exist in the Caribbean (particularly Puerto Rico), Central and South America, and Florida. In at least two of their former haunts the species is now thought to be extinct. Often four or more clutches—of up to 140 eggs each—are laid, usually overnight. This process takes up to three hours, during which time the females and their eggs are vulnerable to predators, including people. An interval of two or three years occurs between each breeding. Hawksbills take at least 30 years to mature to breeding age, a factor that badly affects the replenishment of the population.

Human Interference

Although classed as endangered since 1970, the hawksbill's situation has not improved. Estimates of the worldwide population are impossible to arrive at, but observers who monitor breeding females in various countries are convinced that numbers are falling. Even without human interference sea turtles' eggs and hatchlings face severe predation from wild pigs, monitor lizards, crabs, dogs, and seabirds.

Humans multiply the threats. The sandy beaches needed for turtle nesting are encroached on by building, mainly for tourist facilities. Beach leveling and mechanical raking can destroy nests, while offroad vehicles compact the sand, crushing eggs and producing tire tracks that prevent hatchlings reaching the sea. People simply walking on nesting sites, especially at night, deter nesting female turtles and compact the sand. In addition, artificial lighting along

HAWKSBILL TURTLE

DATA PANEL

Hawksbill turtle

Eretmochelys imbricata

Family: Cheloniidae

World population: Unknown

Distribution: Atlantic, Pacific, and Indian Oceans

Habitat: Shallow tropical and subtropical seas; coral reefs; mangrove bays; estuaries

Size: Length: female 24–37 in (62–94 cm); male up to 39 in (99 cm)

Form: Oval shell with serrated (toothed) edge; dark pattern on amber background

Diet: Sponges and mollusks; algae

Breeding: Up to 140 eggs per clutch; 4–5 clutches per season

Related endangered species: All other sea turtles

Status: IUCN CR

The hawksbill, *like other sea turtles, is toothless and slow-moving, with a protective shell and paddlelike limbs.*

beaches has increased, and hatchlings that would naturally head toward the light on the horizon at sea instead make for the shore lights and die from either dehydration or predation. Other threats come from fishing nets and lines. Some countries insist on turtle-excluder devices on the nets, but they are not always used. Turtles are often killed or mutilated by boat propellers. Pollution by sewage, pesticides, and other chemicals causes further problems. The hawksbill is gravely endangered by the destruction of coral reefs from silting and excavation for building purposes. Illegal capture of the turtles is also widespread.

EX
EW
CR
EN
VU
NT
LC
O

Yellow-blotched Sawback Map Turtle

Graptemys flavimaculata

Map turtles are sometimes called "sawbacks" because of the toothlike projections down the center of their shell. The yellow-blotched sawback increasingly faces threats of pollution in its river habitat.

Of the 12 or so species of map turtle, seven are in decline. The yellow-blotched sawback has the smallest range, living mainly along the Pascagoula River and the Leaf and Chickasawhay Rivers in Mississippi. Exports of map turtles to Britain, Europe, Japan, and Taiwan rose from 325 in 1985 to 84,546 in 1995. It is not known whether the yellow-blotched was among this number, but it has been taken in the past by private and commercial collectors. Many turtles sold in the trade are said to have been farmed, but it is claimed that adults are taken from the wild to replenish breeding stocks.

When the yellow-blotched sawbacks were placed on the IUCN Endangered Species List as Threatened in 1991, many aspects of their behavior and biology were unknown. However, recent studies are providing more information. In the wild females tend to live on mollusks, while males prefer aquatic plants, insects, and larvae. Females become mature when they are about 5 inches (13 cm) long, males when they are about 2.5 inches (6.5 cm) long. In zoo collections females have produced small clutches of between one and five eggs, sometimes laying two or three clutches in a year. The low breeding rate is a problem for a declining species.

DATA PANEL

Yellow-blotched sawback map turtle

Graptemys flavimaculata

Family: Emydidae

World population: Unknown

Distribution: The Pascagoula River system in Mississippi

Habitat: Rivers with slow to medium currents and sandy banks for nesting

Size: Males 2.7–4 in (7–11 cm); females 6–7 in (15–17 cm)

Form: Green-brown shell with yellow blotches; yellow and black stripes on head and limbs; yellowish mark behind each eye; ridge of toothlike projections along back

Diet: Plants and insects

Breeding: Between 1 and 5 eggs per clutch; 2–3 clutches per year

Related endangered species: Barbour's map turtle *(Graptemys barbouri)* LRnt; Cagle's map turtle *(G. caglei)* VU; Escambia map turtle *(G. ernsti)* LRnt; Pascagoula map turtle *(G. gibbonsi)* LRnt; ringed map turtle *(G. oculifera)* EN; Texas map turtle *(G. versa)* LRnt

Status: IUCN EN

Toxic Rivers

Yellow-blotched sawbacks are adapted to living in clean, slow- to moderate-flowing rivers where they use the sandy river banks and sandbars for nesting. They like to bask, making use of rocks or fallen logs for the activity. Most turtle species will only bask in warm, sunny weather, but the yellow-blotched sawbacks will bask even when temperatures are low or when it is raining; This behavior leaves them vulnerable to being killed by thoughtless people who use them as target practice.

However, today, as in the past, the greatest threat is from habitat alteration and destruction. As human settlement spread, trees along the rivers were felled for timber and the land cleared for building. Turtle nesting and basking sites were lost as sandbars and beaches were excavated to improve navigation. Turtle food was swept away during these activities, and some areas of the river became unsuitable for the

turtles because of their greater depth and increased water flow. Industries sprang up along the rivers and began to dump waste products into the water. They killed off food sources, in turn killing off the turtles.

Storm water drains, as well as the construction of dams, levees (embankments to protect against flooding), and flood walls have so altered the riversides that determining the original natural habitat of the yellow-blotched turtle is virtually impossible. In many areas increased recreational use of the rivers and adjacent banks is also obstructing efforts to improve the habitat. Camper vans and offroad vehicles also cause problems for nesting turtles. Some reserves have been established—notably the Pascagoula River Wildlife Management Area, which covers 37,000 acres (15,000 ha) of state-protected land in Mississippi. However, pollution threats from upstream still put the turtles at risk.

The yellow-blotched sawback map turtle *basks on riverbanks, rocks, and logs, a habit that makes it vulnerable to unscrupulous hunters.*

Protective Measures

The turtle's future lies in habitat protection and improvement, especially the reduction of effluent. The species is now protected at both state and federal levels. In some areas of turtle habitat roads are gated and entry prohibited, but signs are ignored by collectors and others. Protection against collecting and deliberate killing requires persuasion and education.

Captive breeding in zoos and private collections has been successful and could help maintain numbers, as long as this goes hand-in-hand with a conservation program for the turtle's river habitat.

Galápagos Giant Tortoise

Geochelone nigra

Before permanent settlers arrived on the Galápagos Islands in the 1830s, there were huge numbers of giant tortoises. Since then habitat destruction and immigrant predators have taken their toll.

Lying off the coast of Ecuador and almost on the equator, the Galápagos Islands achieved lasting fame after the English naturalist Charles Darwin published his theory of evolution in *The Origin of Species* (1859). The book was written after his visit to the islands in 1835. The area was already well known to whalers and other seamen who, between 1789 and 1860, took tortoises to keep on their ships as sources of fresh meat. The tortoises, with water stored in their bladders, would survive on the ships for several months until they were needed. Whaling declined after 1860, when petroleum started to be used instead of whale oil for lighting. Apart from humans, the tortoises had no predators except some birds, which took hatchlings.

Galápagos tortoises are the largest in the world. One male specimen measured 4.3 feet (1.3 m) and weighed about 425 pounds (200 kg). There is considerable variation in the shape of the shell, depending on which island they inhabit, a phenomenon that was noted by Darwin and helped form his theories. Some tortoises have domed shells; others have "saddleback" shells that allow the head to be raised higher. The length of the neck and size of the head also vary; they were considered to be a single species, but scientific study showed that there were 15 different "races" from the various islands, and each one has a third name to distinguish it from others. Three races are now extinct, and some of the others are very rare.

When settlers came to the islands in the 1830s, they brought pigs, goats, dogs, cattle, and burros (donkeys), some of which escaped and began to breed, causing a further decline in tortoise numbers. Pigs and dogs eat eggs and hatchlings; the other animals destroy the vegetation and trample tortoise nests. Rats and fire ants, both introduced species, also eat large numbers of hatchlings.

DATA PANEL

Galápagos giant tortoise

Geochelone nigra

Family: Testudinidae

World population: About 20,000

Distribution: Galápagos Islands, Pacific Ocean

Habitat: Volcanic islands; hot and dry with rocky outcrops; some forested areas with grassy patches

Size: Length: up to 4 ft (1.2 m). Weight: up to 500 lb (227 kg)

Form: Huge tortoise with gray-brown shell and hard-scaled legs; some have domed shells; others are saddleback (resembling a saddle in shape)

Diet: Almost any green vegetation

Breeding: About 7–20 eggs buried in soil

Related endangered species: All subspecies of *Geochelone nigra* are on the IUCN Red List, including the Abingdon Island tortoise *(Geochelone nigra abingdoni)* EW; Duncan Island tortoise *(G. n. ephippium)* EW; Charles Island tortoise *(G. n. galapagoensis)* EX; Hood Island tortoise *(G. n. hoodersis)* CR. The Brazilian giant tortoise *(G. denticulata)* is VU

Status: IUCN VU

COSTA RICA
PANAMA
COLOMBIA
Galápagos Islands (Ecuador)
ECUADOR
PERU

In 1928 a New York Zoological Society expedition collected 180 tortoises and allocated them to zoos as far away as Australia. Some of them have bred to second generation, and one from San Diego zoo was returned to the islands for a captive-breeding program. Following pressure from scientists, the Charles Darwin Foundation was formed in 1959, followed in 1964 by the Charles Darwin Research Station. The islands became a national park, and laws were passed to prevent the removal of any animals.

Long-Term Plans

It is estimated that some islands may need 100 years to recover their vegetation and tortoise populations.

The recovery program instituted by the research station has included collecting eggs from the wild and incubating them artificially, and removing introduced animals. The first young were released in 1970.

Collecting eggs in the wild for incubation has progressed to breeding some tortoises at the research station. The first hatchlings were released in 1975, and in 1991 the first wild-bred hatchling was found on the island. The highlight of the program was the release, early in 2000, of the thousandth tortoise on Espanola.

The tortoise population of the islands has almost doubled in recent years, and laws have been passed to restrict settlement and protect the coastal waters. Quarantine laws forbid the introduction of nonnative plants and animals.

One problem was that some of the races had been reduced to very low numbers, and their lack of genetic diversity was a cause for concern. Even today it is possible that more tortoises may be found on islands where populations are low. This would seem to be the only hope for a tortoise nicknamed Lonesome George, the sole survivor of a race from Pinta Island. He was discovered in 1971 and moved to the station with two females of another race, but as yet no eggs have been produced, and no Pinta female can be found.

Galápagos giant tortoises *are now rare or extinct on many of the islands because of habitat destruction and the introduction of animals that prey on the young or compete with adults for food.*

Jamaican Boa

Epicrates subflavus

Native only to Jamaica, the Jamaican boa—known locally as "yellowsnake"—has suffered from habitat destruction, predation, and deliberate killing. It is now difficult to find in many parts of its former haunts, but sizable captive populations exist in the United States and Europe.

The genus *Epicrates*, to which the Jamaican boa belongs, contains 10 species, one of which lives in South America. The other nine are distributed throughout the West Indies. They are all nonvenomous, using constriction to kill their prey. Although they are harmless, they are, like many snakes, often killed by people out of fear.

The present distribution of the Jamaican boa is patchy as a result of habitat fragmentation and destruction over the years. During the period of European settlement in Jamaica, which began with the Spanish in the 15th century, land was increasingly cleared for agriculture. Farmers brought in pigs, goats, cats, and dogs, and they attracted rats. Mongoose were introduced to control rats, and they started preying on the native fauna, particularly young snakes.

Agriculture is the main source of income in Jamaica, but there is also bauxite mining and tourism, both of which encroach on the boa's natural habitat. There are still some fairly remote, forested areas where the boa thrives, but more roads are being built into the forest, giving easier access to subsistence farmers, woodcutters, charcoal burners, and hunters. Charcoal burning is particularly destructive to the boa's habitat—large amounts of timber are needed to produce a relatively small amount of charcoal.

The Jamaican boa is not in immediate danger of extinction in its main areas, but small, localized populations are at risk. Exactly how many Jamaican boas remain outside captivity is hard to estimate; the boa is difficult to spot in the wild, preferring quiet

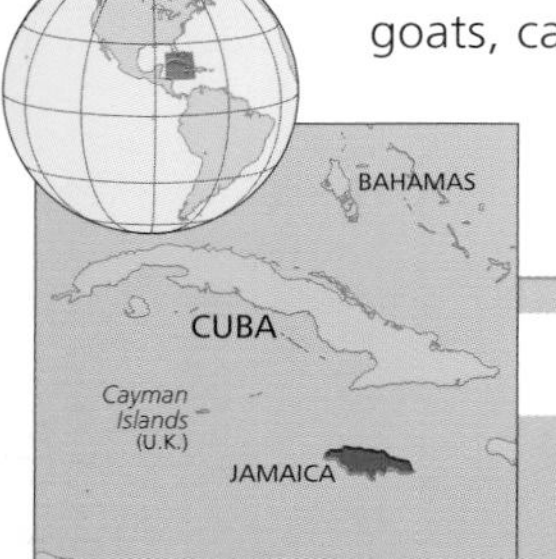

DATA PANEL

Jamaican boa

Epicrates subflavus

Family: Boidae

World population: Unknown

Distribution: Jamaica

Habitat: Mainly forests on honeycomb limestone, although it can be found in moist, tropical forest areas. Safest population in the Blue Mountains in Portland, eastern Jamaica, and the Cockpit Country in Trelawny, northern Jamaica. It is adaptable and has been found in coconut and banana plantations, often near houses

Size: Length: 6–8 ft (1.8–2.4 m)

Form: Long, slender snake with a broad head; anterior part of body yellowish tan or orange to reddish brown, variable black spots become irregular dark bands in the middle of the body; posterior part of body dark blue to black with irregular markings; short dark stripe behind each eye; males smaller and slimmer than females, with prominent pelvic spurs either side of the cloaca (cavity into which alimentary canal, genital, and urinary ducts open)

Diet: Mainly mammals such as rodents and bats, but also birds; young feed mainly on lizards; heat-sensitive pits located on each lip are used to detect warm-blooded prey

Breeding: Livebearer (gives birth to living young). The 5–40 young have pale orange bodies with dark orange to brown crossbands; adult coloration develops at about 18 months

Related endangered species: Cuban tree boa *(Epicrates angulifer)* LRnt; Puerto Rican boa *(E. inornatus)* LRnt; Round Island keel-scaled boa (*Casarea dussumieri*) EN; Asiatic rock python (*Python molurus*) LR

Status: IUCN VU

caves or holes in limestone, and is nocturnal (active at night). Continued fragmentation of the habitat will endanger them further. One population, on Goat Island off Jamaica, has been completely destroyed by mongoose. This island once supported the endangered Jamaican iguana, which is now restricted to a small area in Hellshire on the southern coast. Part of Hellshire has been proposed for national park status. Goat Island may be restored as a habitat, but it would have to be cleared of mongoose first.

Breeding in Captivity

The problems of breeding Jamaican boas in captivity have largely been solved—a number of zoos and private keepers in the United States and Europe hold substantial numbers. The species is known to live for over 20 years in captivity and to produce sizable litters under these conditions. This should provide a good supply of young boas for reintroduction to the wild. Hope Zoo in Kingston, Jamaica, would be an ideal breeding facility, and other zoos, particularly Fort Worth Zoo in Texas, are assisting the staff in Kingston with advice.

Although IUCN listed and designated on CITES Appendix I, the boa's protection in Jamaica has left much to be desired. It was recommended for total protection over 30 years ago, but this was not fully implemented. There is a need to educate and persuade the public to protect this harmless snake. As the population and tourist industry grow, pressure on the land—and the boa's habitat—will increase.

An iridescent sheen *covers the boa's body, particularly when the skin has been newly shed.*

EX
EW
CR
EN
VU
NT
LC
O

Woma Python

Aspidites ramsayi

According to Aboriginal folklore the woma python once roamed Australia in human form, creating the famous Ayers Rock and other mountains in Western Australia during a time known as "dreamtime" in the long-distant past.

The main woma territory is a large area in central Australia that takes in parts of Queensland, Northern Territory, South Australia, and New South Wales. Two populations of woma occur in Western Australia: one in the southwest, the other on the northwestern coast.

Little was known about the species until recently. Its habitat—mainly arid desert and scrubland—was sparsely populated, and the snake was considered rare until herpetologists (those who study reptiles and amphibians) began to observe it and found it to be more common than previously thought. In 1982 the first womas were bred in captivity. Since then it has become a popular species with hobbyists. It is good natured, not too large to accommodate, and reasonably easy to breed in captivity.

Coloration and size vary in woma pythons from different areas. The background color may be drab brown, yellowish, reddish brown, or olive, with darker brown crossbands of varying widths. The head can be light yellow or golden, and is usually unmarked, but in some individuals the juvenile head markings are retained. The snout is pointed, with the upper lip slightly overlapping the lower one. The protruding lip is possibly an adaptation for digging; the woma and its relative, the black-headed python, dig in loose soil using a scooping motion of the head. Unlike other pythons, woma and black-headed pythons do not have heat-detecting pits along the lips to sense warm-blooded prey. Much of their prey is ectothermic (cold-blooded) lizards and, occasionally, snakes.

Studying pythons in the wild in Australia has not been easy because of the vast areas involved, the difficult terrain, and the mainly nocturnal nature of the snakes.

DATA PANEL

Woma python (Ramsay's python)

Aspidites ramsayi

Family: Boidae

World population: Unknown

Distribution: Central Australia: arid regions of Queensland, Northern Territories, South Australia, and Western Australia

Habitat: Arid and semiarid areas, including sand dunes, rocky regions, grasslands, woodlands, and scrub

Size: Length: adults usually 5 ft (1.5 m); occasionally up to 8 ft (2.5 m)

Form: Cylindrical body with short tail and vestiges of hind limbs; eyes with vertically elliptical pupils. Coloration brown, yellowish, reddish brown, or olive with darker brown bands; juveniles more intensively colored. Pointed snout

Diet: Mammals and reptiles (mainly lizards, occasionally snakes)

Breeding: One clutch of 6–19 eggs laid; female incubates eggs

Related endangered species: None

Status: IUCN EN

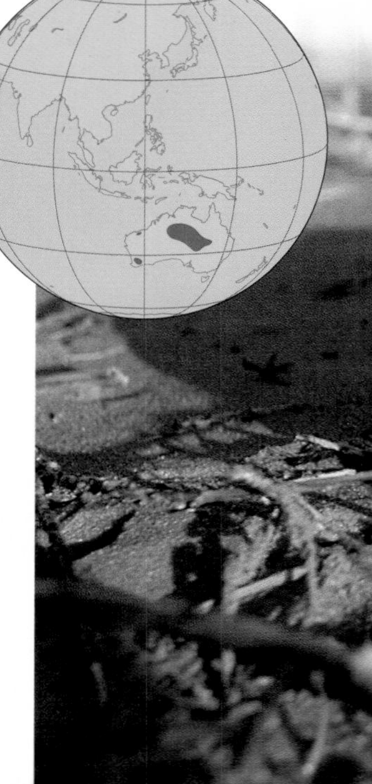

Habitat Loss

Human activity is destroying the outer parts of the woma's range. There is no estimate for total numbers of woma pythons in the wild, but they are known to have declined in certain areas; the last specimen reported in New South Wales was in 1890.

In Queensland land clearance for agriculture and grazing is threatening much suitable habitat; the most severely threatened is the southwestern population of Western Australia. The last confirmed record of woma pythons in the area was in 1987, when a specimen was supplied to the Western Australia Museum.

A large part of woma habitat in Western Australia has been turned over to agriculture, and an area known as the wheatbelt has been increasing for many years. Urban expansion, road construction, and related activities such as crop spraying are all threats. Snakes are also victims of road kills because of their habit of basking on road surfaces. In addition, feral and domestic cats are known to kill snakes, although the extent of predation has not been assessed: An assessment would have to be made if captive-bred young were to be released.

In Captivity

Specimens owned by hobbyists tend to come from the central part of the woma's range. No southwestern womas are held in captivity, although illegally held specimens may exist.

The species as a whole is recognized as being in danger and is listed under government conservation legislation. Even so, snakes are not popular; about 80 percent of Australia's snakes are venomous, and many people are ready to kill snakes of any species, classing them all as deadly.

Herpetologists are trying to investigate the population numbers, particularly of the southwestern form (if it still exists). Conservation bodies and herpetological societies are also trying to increase public awareness and encourage reports of sightings. The Western Australia Amateur Herpetological Society has offered to set up a captive-breeding program at its own cost if any southwestern womas are found and provided that government permission is granted.

The woma, *like other pythons, is nonvenomous; all pythons kill their prey by constriction.*

EX
EW
CR
EN
VU
NT
LC
O

Milos Viper

Macrovipera schweizeri

The endangered Milos viper underwent a big population decline in the late 20th century, but its numbers have now stabilized thanks to better protection of its habitat on the Greek islands of Polyaigos and southern Milos.

The Milos viper occurs only on the islands of Milos, Kimolos, Polyaigos, and Siphnos in the western Cyclades, Greece. Milos, the largest island with an area of 100 square miles (160 sq. km), has the biggest viper population, but suitable habitat has been deteriorating for more than 15 years. The viper's preferred habitat is rocky hillsides with small trees and bushes interspersed with open areas. Much of Kimolos is used for agriculture; it is arid and has little suitable habitat. Polyaigos contains some good areas of habitat since it is not disturbed by people. Siphnos is also used for agriculture. Its viper population has not yet been fully surveyed.

Adult Milos vipers feed mainly on birds, and their young feed on lizards; both avoid areas of dense vegetation, as do their prey. The islands are staging posts for many migratory birds in spring and fall, and some stay there to breed. The vipers are frequent visitors to the watercourses where the birds gather to drink. Although mainly a terrestrial species, the viper is often seen in bushes sheltering from the sun and waiting to ambush birds. Its activity patterns are dictated by the weather. In hot weather it is active mainly at night; in cooler weather it is active during the day. Winter is spent in hibernation, but on mild days the vipers come out to bask.

One unusual feature of the Milos viper is that it lays eggs; other European vipers are livebearers (give birth to live young). Female vipers lay eggs only every other year; breeding may not take place at all if the spring has been cold and they have not fed well. In captivity clutches of up to 10 eggs have been recorded. Eggs and young are eaten by predators such as rats and feral (wild) cats or destroyed by human activity. The cats also kill adult vipers.

Balancing Act

Milos has a population of fewer than 5,000 people concentrated mostly in the eastern corner of the island. The vipers live on the sparsely populated, more mountainous west. Other islands have fewer people. The current viper population on Milos is estimated at fewer than 2,500; Polyaigos and Kimolos each have even smaller numbers. This may sound a lot, but unless they can maintain a balance between births and deaths, they will become extinct.

Habitat destruction has been ongoing on Milos for several years. Quarrying for minerals and cement production has laid

DATA PANEL

Milos viper (Cyclades blunt-nosed viper)

Macrovipera schweizeri

Family: Viperidae

World population: About 3,000

Distribution: Western Cyclades islands, Greece

Habitat: Mostly rocky areas with open spaces between bushes

Size: Length: 30 in (75 cm)

Form: Heavy-bodied snake; 2 hollow fangs on short maxilla (upper jaw); red-brown blotches on lighter background

Diet: Birds and lizards

Breeding: Between 8 and 10 eggs laid every other year

Related endangered species: Several species of viper in Europe and Asia, including Latifi's viper *(Vipera latifi)* VU of Iran and mountain viper *(V. albizona)* EN of Turkey

Status: IUCN EN

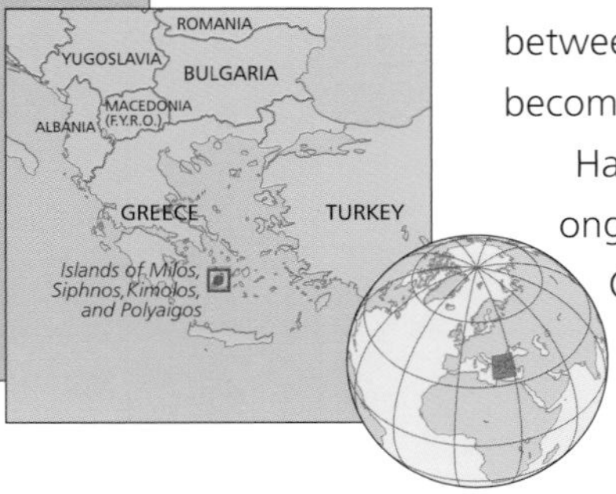

The Milos viper's *venom is quite strong, but few people are bitten, and no fatalities have been recorded.*

waste much of the suitable viper habitat in the west. The mineral industry on Milos is vital to the national economy, and expansion of the business is planned. Traffic supports the industry, and road kills are becoming more common, particularly at night in summer. Wildlife was not moved before the quarrying began, and spoiled areas have not been restored. Natural restoration takes several years, even if the new growth is not grazed; overgrazing by sheep and goats is an additional problem in some areas.

Until recently Milos has not been badly affected by tourism, but now tourist numbers have increased, and a second airport is planned. House building and land clearance for agriculture are also changing the viper's habitat. Tourism may prove a mixed blessing, possibly slowing down industrial expansion, but it might also destroy more habitat and increase disturbance. Vipers found near tourist areas might be deliberately eradicated so that they do not deter visitors. In the recent past vipers were deliberately killed. Until 1977 trappers could claim 10 drachmas (then about 15 U.S. cents) from the authorities for each viper caught, but in 1981 a presidential decree on wildlife protection outlawed the collection or killing of all wildlife. A cause of decline had been collection by hobbyists and by people intending to sell the vipers. Substantial numbers were taken in the 1980s, but collecting has been reduced in recent years.

In 1985 creation of a biogenetic reserve was recommended after a report by the Societas Europaea Herpetologica (SEH). Another report by the SEH in 1986 proposed greater control of quarrying, the employment of game wardens, and education programs to inform the public and so protect the species. A survey between 1993 and 1997 examined the viper's ecology, population, and threats to its habitat. Recommendations were made and, although the government was slow to respond, protection is now afforded by the European network of protected sites. Most of the areas considered for conservation are of archaeological importance and do not contain any viper habitats. However, habitat protection is vital for the future of the Milos viper.

EX
EW
CR
EN
VU
NT
LC
O

Chinese Alligator

Alligator sinensis

The Chinese alligator is one of the smaller crocodilians (large, predatory reptiles of the order Crocodilia), and possibly the rarest. Its range has been restricted by expanding human populations in China, and it is now endangered, although farmed specimens are restoring numbers overall.

Like all crocodilians, the Chinese alligator is an efficient predator that is well adapted to its lifestyle. It is reclusive, feeding mainly at night and spending six to seven months hibernating in burrows. The burrow system is complex, often having ventilation holes up to the surface. The alligators' habits, together with their efficient camouflage, mean that they can often go undetected even when they are near human habitation.

Once widespread, the species is now mainly restricted to 13 small protected areas within Anhui Chinese Alligator National Nature Reserve, an area of 167 square miles (433 sq. km). The alligators' association with the dragons of Chinese mythology offers no protection. Their habitat is in an area of dense human population that has been heavily cultivated, principally by draining swamps and clearing vegetation. Pressure to expand cultivation is growing as the population increases.

The Chinese alligator does not eat humans, but is feared by local people and considered an expensive nuisance because of its burrowing, which destroys irrigation dams. Although the alligator's diet is mainly snails and mussels—the broad teeth are adapted to crushing mollusk shells—they will take fish and ducks, which brings them into conflict with humans.

The alligator is a protected species, but that does not stop it from being killed and sold for meat and medicinal use. The meat and skins are not as sought-after as those of some other species; the skin is difficult to tan due to the large osteoderms (bony plates) under the scales. Its lower value means that it is not worth hunting the alligators on a commercial basis. However, occasional kills remove a pest and earn a little money.

DATA PANEL

Chinese alligator

Alligator sinensis

Family: Alligatoridae

World population: More than 10,000, but possibly only 200 in the wild

Distribution: Lower Yangtze River in China

Habitat: Slow-moving freshwater rivers and streams; lakes, ponds, and swamps

Size: Length: up to 6 ft (2 m). Weight: up to 85 lb (40 kg)

Form: Similar to the American alligator, but smaller and with a more tapered head. Snout is slightly upturned near the nostrils. Color is dark brown to black. Young carry bright-yellow crossbands that fade with age

Diet: Snails, mussels, fish, and ducks

Breeding: Clutch of 10–40 eggs per year laid under mounds of decaying vegetation. Average clutch size in captivity is 15 eggs. Females may occasionally miss breeding one year. Incubation about 70 days

Related endangered species: Black caiman *(Melanosuchus niger)* LRcd

Status: IUCN CR

NORTH KOREA
SOUTH KOREA
CHINA

Surviving Populations

When the species was added to the IUCN listing in 1965, the estimated wild population was 50 specimens. Today the figure is only about 200, of which only about 50 are mature adults. These live in the lower Yangtze River, including in the Anhui Reserve. A few live in other reserves and possibly in scattered isolated areas along the Yangtze River's tributaries.

There are more alligators in captivity than in the wild. Captive-breeding programs have been successful; starting in the early 1960s with 200 wild alligators and 780 wild eggs, numbers increased to just over 4,000 by 1991. Breeding centers have been set up in China, and Chinese alligators have been bred at several American and European zoos. Currently the number of alligators in establishments is more than 10,000, most of these in China. Outside of that country there are several hundred in zoos and a few in private collections. Space is limited in zoos, however. The young will live together quite well up to the age of three or four years; but as they grow, fights and cannibalism can become a problem. Breeding from second-generation animals is not carried out for these reasons.

The Chinese alligator's *survival in the wild depends on a change in people's attitudes and greater protection of the animal's habitat.*

Future Prospects

It may seem odd that although the wild alligators are listed in CITES Appendix I, the farmed specimens are in Appendix II, which means that they can enter trade. The original idea was to produce them for meat and for the European pet market, although it is doubtful if the demand in Europe would be great enough to make breeding worthwhile. However, the industry provides much-needed jobs for many people.

The Chinese alligator has been proven to thrive in captivity. Females are mature at between four and five years, which makes them ideal for captive breeding. Its longevity and reasonable clutch size mean that wild areas could be repopulated if the habitat was not being constantly threatened.

American Crocodile

Crocodylus acutus

The American crocodile has a much wider distribution than some other crocodiles and alligators. Although in the United States it is restricted to southern Florida, it is found in 16 other countries. Like the alligator, it has been hunted to supply the lucrative trade in leather made from crocodile skin.

In the United States crocodiles live in the tidal marshes in the Everglades along Florida Bay and in the Florida Keys. The American crocodile is also found in western Mexico through Central America down to northeastern Peru and into Venezuela. It occurs on some Caribbean islands, mainly Cuba (which has the largest wild population) and also Jamaica, Haiti, and the Dominican Republic. In all these countries crocodile populations have declined.

Crocodiles are fairly adaptable; they are excellent swimmers, they can travel considerable distances overland, and they can live in fresh or salt water. However, urban development—for example in Dade and Monroe counties, Florida—has reduced their habitat. One population has taken refuge in brackish water cooling channels at Turkey Point nuclear power station in Florida.

Like alligators, crocodiles do not usually attack humans unless they or their nests are disturbed. In Florida the crocodiles and their nests are strictly protected; killing, feeding, or disturbing them in any way is illegal.

Crocodiles are good burrowers, excavating deep holes for shelter and nesting. In the absence of suitable soil they will cover the eggs with a mound of loose vegetation. Eggs and youngsters are vulnerable to predators. Racoons in the United States dig up their nests, as do teiid lizards in Central America. Flooding can also destroy nests before the eggs hatch.

DATA PANEL

American crocodile

Crocodylus acutus

Family: Crocodylidae

World population: Unknown

Distribution: Southern Florida, Central America, Peru, and Venezuela

Habitat: Fresh and salt water; swamps, rivers, lakes, reservoirs, and mangrove swamps

Size: Length: male 16–19 ft (5–6 m); female up to 16 ft (5 m). Reports of specimens 22 ft (7 m) long in Central America. Weight: 700–800 lb (318–363 kg)

Form: Large lizardlike reptiles with longer and narrower snouts than alligators and a body that is not as well armored. The fourth tooth on each side of the lower jaw is visible when the mouth is closed. Coloration is green-gray or gray-tan with duskymarkings. Adults have a prominent swelling in front of each eye

Diet: Fish, crabs, turtles, birds, and small mammals; can attack livestock

Breeding: Clutches of 20–60 eggs are laid in excavated holes or buried in mounds of loose vegetation. Incubation takes about 3 months

Related endangered species: Orinoco crocodile *(Crocodylus intermedius)* CR; Philippines crocodile *(C. mindorensis)* CR; marsh or mugger crocodile *(C. palustris)* VU; Cuban crocodile *(C. rhombifer)* CR; Siamese crocodile *(C. siamensis)* CR

Status: IUCN VU

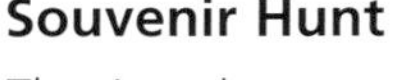

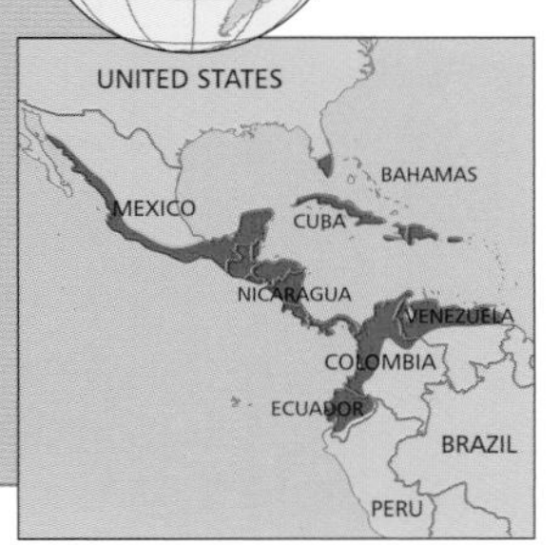

Souvenir Hunt

The American crocodile is threatened both by urban development and by other forms of habitat destruction. In Ecuador, for example, mangroves have been cleared for shrimp aquaculture. Crocodiles are also sometimes killed out of fear or because they are seen as a threat to

livestock. Illegal hunting for the trade in skins or for making tourist souvenirs is common. Other threats include accidental capture in fishing nets, tropical storms, and overfishing; fish form a large part of their diet.

The American crocodile *feeds in the water (often floating at the surface to lie in wait for prey) and comes onto land to bask in the sun and to lay eggs.*

Conservation

The Crocodile Specialist Group (CSG) consists of experts and other interested parties who advise the Species Survival Commission of the IUCN on crocodilian conservation. Operating from the Florida Museum of Natural History, the group monitors crocodile populations and draws up conservation programs; by 1971 the CSG had set up a conservation program for all 23 crocodilian species throughout the world. Monitoring the crocodiles is a mammoth task. The most detailed study has been that of the Florida population, but in several countries very little up-to-date information is available, and there is a need for more fieldwork. The CSG is funded by voluntary donations, so funds are not always sufficient to do what is needed.

The American crocodile was listed as Endangered in 1979, and a recovery plan was initiated by the United States Fish and Wildlife Service in 1984 to cover aspects such as habitat protection and captive-breeding programs. Captive breeding for the skin trade and restocking exists in six countries, but recent reduced demand for skins may remove the financial incentive for this to continue. Few zoos have captive-breeding programs, although one notable success was the hatching of 10 young crocodiles in 1996 at Cleveland Metroparks Zoo. In Venezuela protection and releases of captive-bred stock are aiding recovery.

Florida's crocodile population is slowly increasing, but in several countries (such as El Salvador and Haiti) they are still declining. There is an urgent need for restocking of the wild populations.

EX
EW
CR
EN
VU
NT
LC
O

Gharial

Gavialis gangeticus

One of the largest crocodilian species, the gharial (or gavial) came close to extinction in the 1970s. Traditionally, gharials were not threatened by humans since they were regarded as sacred. Today they have disappeared from much of their original range. Conservation programs increased numbers in the 1990s, but since then they have fallen again.

An unusual crocodilian, the gharial's common name comes from the Indian word "ghara," a pot, and refers to the bulbous growth on the male's snout. The growth is thought to act as a resonator when the male calls, or it may be used for recognition of males by females.

The gharial's distinctive narrow, tooth-lined snout, which seems at odds with the heavy body, is an adaptation to a diet of fish. The snout can be quickly slashed sideways, and the razor-sharp, slightly angled teeth are able to gain a firm grip on the slippery fish. Large specimens sometimes seize larger prey such as mammals, but youngsters feed on aquatic invertebrates and small creatures such as frogs.

Gharials spend much of their time in water, crawling onto land to bask or nest. Once out of water, their legs cannot raise the body off the ground, but they are capable of rapid movement by slithering on the belly. Unlike most crocodilians, gharials do not transport hatchlings from the nest to water, possibly because of their jaw structure, but the mothers do guard their young once they have hatched and reached water.

Population Decline

The gharial was once found in the major rivers and their tributaries in the northern parts of the Indian subcontinent, namely the Brahmaputra (India, Bhutan, Bangladesh); the Indus (Pakistan); the Ganges (Nepal and India); the Mahandi (India); and the Narayoni River and

DATA PANEL

Gharial (gavial)

Gavialis gangeticus

Family: Gavialidae

World population: 182 known

Distribution: Northern Indian subcontinent

Habitat: Largely aquatic; calmer areas of deep rivers with sandbanks for nesting

Size: Length: male 19–22 ft (6–7 m); female about 16 ft (5 m)

Form: Typical crocodilian shape. Elongated, narrow snout with many interlocking, sharp teeth. Males have a bulbous growth on the end of the snout.

Adult color: uniform olive gray, sometimes with brownish blotches or bands, especially on the tail. Juveniles have dark spots and crossbands on a yellow-brown background

Diet: Fish; sometimes small mammals

Breeding: Clutch of 30–50 eggs buried in loose sand; eggs take 12–13 weeks to hatch

Related endangered species: None

Status: IUCN CR

its tributaries (Nepal), with smaller populations in the Kaladan and Irrawaddy Rivers in Myanmar (Burma). Today the remaining populations are in India and Nepal, with perhaps a few specimens in isolated areas.

The gharial's decline has been due to human activity. Settlements set up along the rivers have destroyed or disturbed breeding areas. Fishermen regard the gharials as direct competitors and destroyers of fishing nets. Furthermore, gharials are reputed to be man-eaters. While they do not attack people, they are thought to scavenge on human remains in the river (traditionally corpses are placed in the Ganges during funeral ceremonies). In some areas people hunt gharials for meat, and the eggs and body parts are also used in traditional medicine.

Chances of Survival

The gharial benefited from a recovery plan set up in India in the 1970s to prevent poaching losses. Nine protected areas were established along the Ganges and its tributaries, and six captive-breeding and ranching centers were started, where eggs were taken from the wild to be hatched and raised in captivity. Several thousand young gharials have been released into the wild; this has steadied the decline in some areas. At smaller sites, however, numbers have not increased since youngsters do not always remain in the release area. In Nepal captive breeding and releases have produced only a small improvement in numbers.

The gharial has recently become even rarer in India and Nepal and is almost extinct in Pakistan. It remains at risk from habitat degradation, fishing, and hunting. The wild population was estimated at 182 in 2006. There is a shortage of suitable release sites in the protected areas, and the high cost of captive breeding and protection is also a problem. Ideally, youngsters should not be released until they are about five years old. However, the cost of feeding and caring for them means that some have been prematurely released, which reduces their chances of survival in the wild.

The gharial *is distinguished by its long, slender snout and sharp-toothed jaws.*

Gila Monster

Heloderma suspectum

In spite of its sluggish, awkward movement, the Gila monster can turn quickly if attacked. Its powerful venomous bite has made it the subject of many myths.

Venomous bites are usually associated with snakes, but the Gila monster and its close relative, the Mexican beaded lizard, are the only two venomous lizards in the world. The Gila monster, sometimes referred to as the Aztec lizard because it featured in paintings by the Aztec people of the ancient Mexican-Indian empire, has been the subject of many myths. They are supposed to be unable to pass out body waste and so to have poisonous breath. They are also reputed to spit venom, have a venomous tongue, and to be impossible to kill. Their venomous bite is real; the remainder untrue.

The Gila monster's bite is surprisingly quick and powerful, considering the animal generally moves in a sluggish, awkward way. Once it has its prey in its jaws, the Gila will then hang onto it, using a chewing motion to introduce venom into the prey's wounds. The venom is contained in glands in either side of the lower jaw from where it flows along grooves in some of the teeth. These pink glands contrast with the dark mouth lining, possibly acting as a visible warning when the mouth is open in a threat display. There is some debate over whether the venom is mainly for defense or for subduing prey. Gila venom is not highly toxic to humans, though bites have been described as extremely painful: Symptoms can include severe localized pain, sweating, breathing difficulty, blurred vision, swelling, vomiting, and reduced blood pressure. However, the Gila monster only uses venom in about a third of all bites.

Desert Destruction

Much of the Gila monster's habitat has been reduced by human encroachment into desert areas. Like many other creatures, it has been affected by urban development, agriculture, and industry. Construction

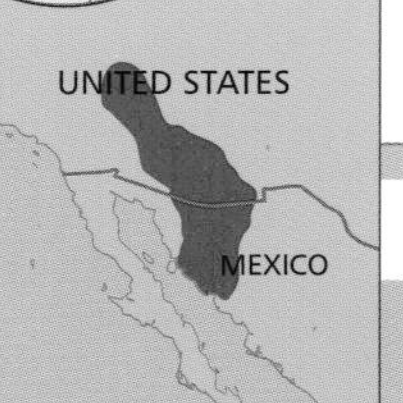

DATA PANEL

Gila monster (Aztec lizard)

Heloderma suspectum

Family: Helodermatidae

World population: Several thousand

Distribution: Southwestern U.S. (Sonoran, Chihuahan, and Mojave Deserts)

Habitat: Desert and semiarid regions among sand, gravel, rocks, and vegetation such as saguaro, cholla, and prickly pear; often shelters in burrows of other animals

Size: Length: 18–24 in (45–60 cm)

Form: Heavy-bodied; short, fat tail used to store fat; short, powerful limbs for digging; black face; scales small and beadlike; coloration and pattern vary: mixture of black, orange, yellow, and pink markings in irregular bars, spots, or blotches

Diet: Eggs, small mammals, and birds

Breeding: One clutch of up to 12 eggs

Related endangered species: Mexican beaded lizard *(Heloderma horridum)* LC

Status: IUCN NT

work, use of offroad vehicles, and other human activities destroy the burrows where the Gila monster spends much of its time, particularly during the cold winter months. One study estimates that the Gila spends 90 percent of the year in burrows. The Gila's slow metabolism means that it does not need to feed as often as smaller, more active lizards. Its prey consists of eggs, small mammals, and young birds, usually swallowed whole, which provide moisture as well as sustenance. Once fed, the Gila rests until another meal is needed or it wants to bask in the sun.

Deliberate killing of the Gila has taken its toll on the species. Gilas are often killed out of fear, bravado, or simply ignorance. However, not all people fear Gila monsters. There has been a huge interest in reptile-keeping in the past few decades, and Gilas are now kept by many hobbyists. Many have been taken from the wild, even though it is now illegal to do so.

Protection

Some towns have municipal ordinances against keeping Gilas. In Arizona state legislation protecting Gilas was enacted as far back as 1952 but was not always enforced. The species is listed on CITES Appendix II, which means that only Gilas bred in captivity can be exported, and they require appropriate licenses. There has recently been pressure to upgrade Gilas to CITES Appendix I to legislate against any trade in the species.

In some areas only authorized people can handle "nuisance" Gilas that turn up on people's property. There are guidelines on where they can then be released so that they are not left in unsuitable habitats or too far away from their home range.

Some areas of habitat are now reserves, and many zoos have groups, although not all are able to breed. Since captive-breeding is possible, numbers can be increased, but habitat loss remains a problem. Recent scientific research has shown that the Gila monster's venom contains a substance useful in the treatment of diabetes.

The Gila monster's *differently colored scales and black face can be effective camouflage. The colors may also act as a warning to other animals.*

What is an Amphibian?

As their name implies, amphibians typically have a dual lifestyle, living part of their life in water and part on land. While this is true of many of the approximately 6,260 species that live on earth today, there are many amphibians for which it is not. Some are wholly aquatic, never leaving water throughout their lives; others are wholly terrestrial and spend no part of their life in water. All, however, wholly depend on wet or damp conditions, and much of the diversity of amphibians lies in the many remarkable ways in which they exploit sources of water. All amphibians have a three-stage life cycle, comprising egg, larval, and adult stages. The larval stage of frogs and toads is called a tadpole. Here again, there is a good deal of diversity among species, and one of these stages may even appear to be lost. In some species, for example, the larval stage is completed inside the egg, which hatches to produce a miniature adult. In other species the larval form is retained into adulthood—a phenomenon called pedomorphosis—so that the adult stage is essentially a giant larva.

The dependence of amphibians on damp or wet conditions stems from the fact that at no stage in their life cycle do they have a protective covering that prevents them losing water by evaporation. Amphibian eggs lack the tough shells of reptile and bird eggs, and the skin of both larvae and adults is thin and lacks scales or an impervious outer layer.

Amphibians are ectothermic (cold-blooded), meaning that they derive their body heat from their environment, sometimes by basking in the sun. As a result, their level of activity depends very much on the weather; on cold days they are sluggish and inactive. Temperature also affects the time that it takes an egg to develop into a larva and a larva to transform into an adult; both processes are faster in warm conditions. Ectothermic animals need very little food and can survive for very long periods without eating. When they do have abundant food, they store much of it as fat. That enables them to survive periods when conditions are adverse, such as during the cold winter or the dry summer. Some desert-living amphibians can survive for over a year buried in the ground.

Metamorphosis

A feature of amphibians' life history that makes them quite distinct from other vertebrates is metamorphosis, the change in form that they undergo from larva to adult. It involves enormous anatomical changes, especially in frogs and toads, which acquire four legs and lose a tail, as well as radical structural and physiological changes in the way that they breathe and move. In most amphibians the larvae acquire oxygen from water, through external gills, but the adults breathe air by means of lungs. Almost all amphibians, however, meet part of their oxygen needs through their skin.

Diverse Locomotion

Amphibians are remarkably diverse in terms of the way that they move, and many species have several methods of locomotion. Aquatic salamanders and newts swim quite like fish, undulating their very flexible bodies from side to side. Frogs and toads swim quite differently; they have short, rigid bodies, no tail, and swim by beating their legs. Many amphibians are adapted for burrowing into the soil. Burrowing frogs and toads have horny, spadelike structures on their feet that enable them to shift the soil. The caecilians, lacking legs, burrow like earthworms. Tree frogs are very good climbers, equipped with adhesive disks on the ends of their fingers and toes that enable them to cling to the smoothest vertical surfaces. Many frogs are spectacular leapers, their enlarged hindlimbs enabling them to jump many times their body length.

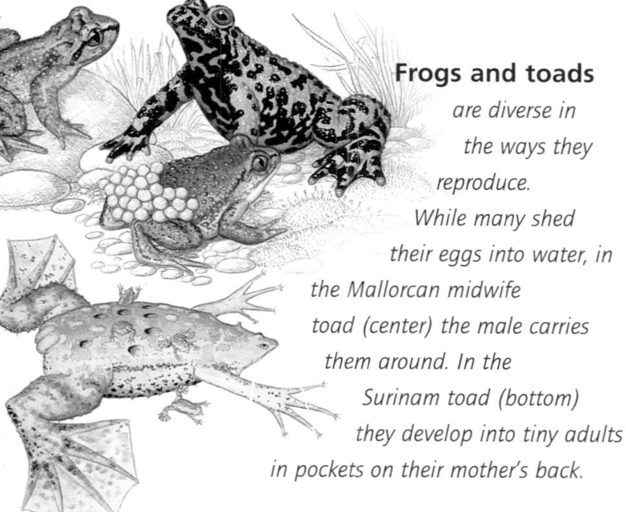

Frogs and toads *are diverse in the ways they reproduce. While many shed their eggs into water, in the Mallorcan midwife toad (center) the male carries them around. In the Surinam toad (bottom) they develop into tiny adults in pockets on their mother's back.*

A few frogs are capable of a simple form of flight. By spreading their long, webbed toes like parachutes, they can glide while jumping from tree to tree.

Diverse Reproduction

Diversity is also a feature of amphibian reproductive patterns. Most frogs and toads, and the more primitive salamanders, have external fertilization, the male shedding sperm onto the eggs immediately after they are laid. Most salamanders and all caecilians have internal fertilization. While caecilians have a penislike intromittent organ, salamanders and newts transfer their sperm in capsules called spermatophores, a form of mating unique among vertebrates but similar to that of a variety of invertebrates.

Many amphibians have evolved remarkable forms of parental care. They include frogs in which the eggs develop in pockets in their mother's skin, frogs in which the father carries tadpoles from pool to pool, salamanders that give birth to fully developed young, and even frogs that lay their eggs in foam nests hanging from trees, where they can be kept out of reach from predators.

The powerful hind legs *of most frogs and toads enable them to leap large distances to escape predators.*

Three Amphibian Orders

Amphibians are divided into three orders that are very different in anatomy, lifestyle, and behavior. The largest order, containing 5,532 species in 29 families, is the Anura; they are the frogs and toads. The order Caudata (also called the Urodela) are tailed amphibians, the salamanders and newts, of which there are 552 species in 10 families. The smallest order, containing 176 species in five families, is the Gymnophiona (also called the Caecilia). They are wormlike creatures that lack limbs and live underground or in the mud at the bottom of pools and streams.

The History of Amphibians

Amphibians occupy a special place in the evolution of animals, being the first vertebrates to live on land. They are often referred to as the ancestors of the reptiles, but that is misleading because modern amphibians look nothing at all like their ancient ancestors, which also gave rise to the reptiles. Some of the earliest amphibians, living in the Devonian period 360 million years ago, were massive, heavily built creatures as large as crocodiles. For a time they were the dominant creatures on the land, very different from the situation today, when amphibians are generally small, delicately built creatures. The ancestors of amphibians were the lobefinned fish, which breathed air from the water surface using lungs rather than gills.

Unfortunately, there are very few fossil remains of the earliest amphibians, so it is unclear quite how or why the transition from living in water to living on land came about. The lack of fossils also means that it is by no means certain that the three living groups of amphibians are descended from a common ancestor; it is quite possible that each evolved, independently, from the fish.

Why Are Amphibians at Risk?

Amphibians are subject to the same kind of threats as other animals, but certain features of their way of life make them particularly vulnerable. Amphibians throughout the world are threatened by habitat destruction, pollution, climate change, and in some instances, by overexploitation.

Amphibians are more threatened by habitat loss than many other species that depend on water because they depend more on small bodies of water—such as ponds and streams—and less on larger lakes and rivers, where they cannot coexist with fish. Small ponds, streams, marshes, and wetlands do not have the economic or recreational value that helps ensure the protection of lakes and rivers.

Many amphibians breed in ponds or streams that dry up for part of the year. They make ideal breeding habitat because they cannot support populations of fish and other wholly aquatic predators that would otherwise prey on their eggs and larvae. However, such ephemeral water bodies are particularly susceptible to climate change, and there are a number of parts of the world where prolonged drought has led to major declines in populations simply because

The earliest amphibians *were much larger and more heavily built than their living descendants. Ancestral amphibians from the Triassic period (225 to 190 million years ago) included Mastodonsaurus (top), which was 13 feet (4 m) long, Diadectes (middle), which was 10 feet (3 m) long, and Eryops (bottom), which was 5 feet (1.5 m) long.*

they have been unable to maintain an adequate reproductive output.

Another factor that particularly affects amphibians is increased levels of ultraviolet radiation resulting from the thinning of the ozone layer in the upper atmosphere. The eggs of many amphibians are laid in open, shallow pools, where the sunlight is intense, and ultraviolet radiation causes major mortality among them because it breaks up DNA, preventing successful cell division and growth.

In the last few years a new threat to amphibians has emerged: infectious disease. In particular, a virus has caused mass mortalities in Britain and North America, and a fungus has caused a disease called chytridiomycosis in Australia, Central, North, and South America, and Europe. Quite why these disease outbreaks have occurred is not clear. One possibility is that alteration of the habitat by humans facilitates the spread of disease. Another is that one or more other factors, such as climate change or increased UV radiation, has adversely affected the immune system of amphibians so that they can no longer withstand diseases to which they were once immune.

The Situation Today

In 1990 just over 4,000 species of amphibians were known to biologists; today the figure is at least 6,260. Of these, 37.9 percent were considered to be Critically Endangered, Endangered, Vulnerable, or Near Threatened in 2008. It is ironic that at a time when amphibians have been disappearing at an unparalleled rate, scientists are discovering new species in large numbers. One reason for this is that alarm about recent declines among amphibians has motivated biologists to document amphibian diversity more accurately before they disappear. Many recently described species are the result of exploration into remote parts of the world where amphibians have not been fully studied before.

Not all "new" species have been found in this way, however. There are several amphibian species that were previously thought to be single, wide-ranging species; as the result of the application of modern genetic techniques, they have been found to be made up of genetically distinct species that are similar in appearance. Recent declines among amphibian numbers, many of which have occurred in supposedly "safe" areas such as nature reserves, have prompted a major global initiative. The IUCN is seeking to assess the status of all amphibians, to document the declines, and to determine the nature of the threats they are facing.

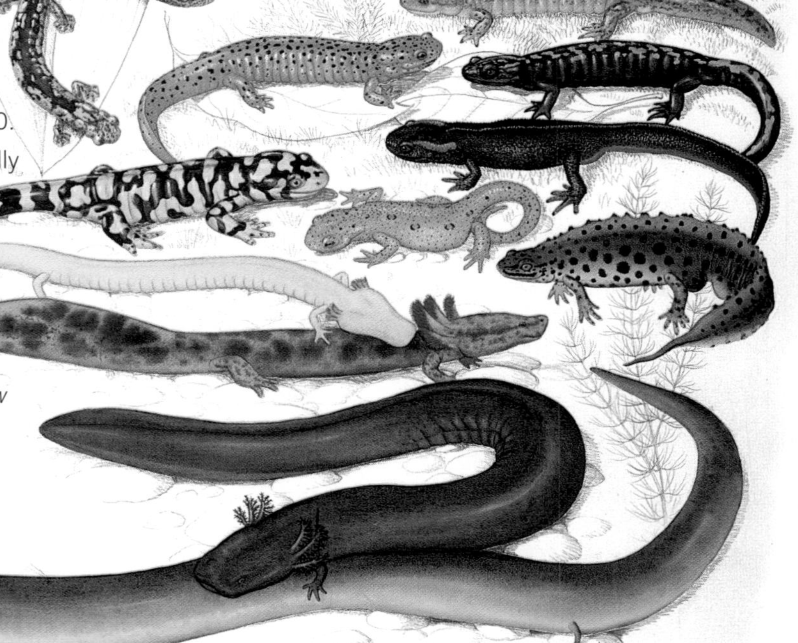

The tailed amphibians *(salamanders and newts) show diversity in their size, color, shape, and lifestyle. They range from tiny, wholly terrestrial animals like the arboreal, 2-inch (5-cm) Bolitoglossa (top left) to the wholly aquatic 30-inch (76-cm) Amphiuma (bottom), which resembles a large eel.*

EX
EW
CR
EN
VU
NT
LC
O

Japanese Giant Salamander

Andrias japonicus

Restricted to just two mountainous areas, the Japanese giant salamander's mountain stream habitat is under threat from damming and deforestation. Collection has also depleted numbers. Fortunately, the salamander is now fully protected by international trade restrictions.

The Japanese giant salamander and its close relative the Chinese giant salamander from China and Taiwan are the largest salamanders in the world. An inhabitant of mountain streams with clear, cool water, the Japanese giant salamander is similar in anatomy and habits to the hellbender of North America, and the two Asian species are sometimes known as Oriental hellbenders.

The Japanese giant salamander has a heavily built, slightly compressed body and a flat head, with small eyes and nostrils at the tip of its snout. Its skin is rough and warty, with many wrinkles and folds, giving the impression that its body is too small for its skin. Two prominent folds run along the whole length of its body. The tail, which makes up about a quarter of its total length, is flattened from side to side and has a fin along the upper side. The limbs are small and also slightly flattened. In color the salamander is reddish or grayish brown with a darker mottled pattern, and it is paler on the underside. Males and females are similar in size and appearance, except that the male develops a swollen cloaca (cavity into which the alimentary canal, genital, and urinary ducts open) during the breeding season.

The Japanese giant salamander is a retiring animal by day, hiding under rocks or in a burrow. It emerges at night in search of food, which includes fish, worms, and crustaceans such as crayfish. It has an unusual arrangement of jawbones and muscles, which enables it to suck its prey into its mouth. It requires the clean, well-oxygenated water that is found only in fast-flowing streams and so is confined to altitudes between 980 and 3,300 feet (300 and 1,000 m). The Chinese giant salamander is found in a similar habitat, but also occurs in mountain lakes.

DATA PANEL

Japanese giant salamander

Andrias japonicus

Family: Cryptobranchidae

World population: Unknown

Distribution: Southern Japan; islands of Honshu and Kyushu

Habitat: Rocky mountain streams with clear, fast-flowing, and well-oxygenated water

Size: Length: 8–56 in (20–140 cm)

Form: Large salamander; long, flattened body; rough, warty skin with many wrinkles and folds. Laterally compressed tail with dorsal (back) fin. Broad, flat head; small eyes. Reddish or grayish brown on upper body; paler below

Diet: Fish, worms, and crustaceans

Breeding: Fall (August–September)

Related endangered species: Chinese giant salamander *(Andrias davidianus)* CR

Status: IUCN NT

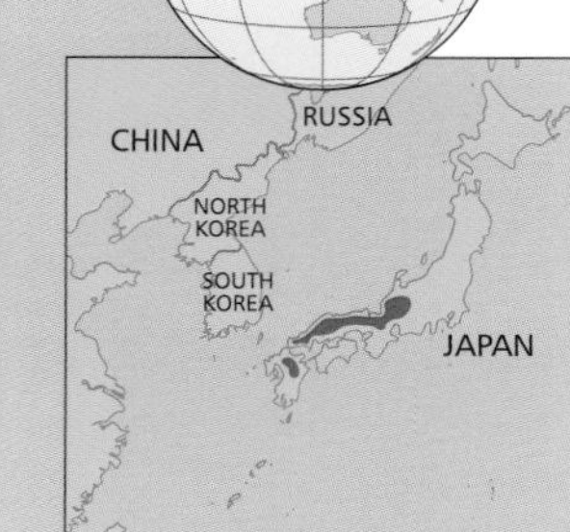

Breathing through the Skin

The giant salamanders show a form of pedomorphosis, retaining many aspects of the larval form into adult life. Unlike some pedomorphic salamanders, however, giant salamanders lose their external gills when they are about 18 months old and about 4.5 inches (12 cm) in length. Thereafter they rely on their skin to absorb oxygen from the water. The skin of giant salamanders contains a higher density of blood capillaries than most salamanders, and the many wrinkles and folds in the skin increase the surface area over which oxygen is absorbed. When resting, the salamanders sway slowly from side to side; this serves to gently stir up the water, ensuring that well-oxygenated water is always close to their skin.

Paternal Care

Breeding begins in the fall (August to September). The male Japanese giant salamander plays a more active role than is true for most salamanders. He digs a pit in the gravel on a stream bed, defending his territory aggressively against rival males. At the same time, he displays to attract a female into the pit. The female lays 400 to 600 eggs in strings that are between 7 and 60 feet (2 and 18 m) in length, and the male sheds sperm onto them. Mating attracts the attention of other, usually smaller males, who enter the nest and also shed sperm on the eggs. After mating, the female leaves the male, who guards the eggs until they hatch, after about two months. The newly hatched larvae disperse from the nest and reach maturity at about three years of age. Giant salamanders are very long-lived; one animal, in Amsterdam Zoo, lived to be 52 years old.

Protected Species

The large size of the Japanese giant salamander, together with its specific habitat requirements, means that it was never an abundant creature. As a result, it has been particularly badly affected by deforestation and the damming of rivers, activities that destroy the clear, well-oxygenated streams it prefers.

Japanese giant salamanders have also been collected in the past and sent to many museums, aquaria, and zoos throughout the world. However, this kind of trade is now tightly controlled, the species having been given full protection under the CITES treaty.

The Japanese giant salamander *loses its external gills at about 18 months, when it is about 4.5 inches (12 cm) in length.*

EX
EW
CR
EN
VU
NT
LC
O

Olm

Proteus anguinus

A bizarre, permanently aquatic salamander that lives almost entirely underground, the olm is vulnerable to a variety of factors that threaten its restricted and specialized habitat.

The olm is a strange and obscure amphibian. It is highly adapted to a habitat of underground streams, pools, and lakes, and shows a classic example of pedomorphism. This is an evolutionary change that results in the retention of juvenile characteristics in the adult form. The species does not exist as a terrestrial, lung-breathing salamander. During the course of its normal pattern of development the olm has become "frozen" in the larval stage, retaining the large, feathery external gills and laterally compressed tail, which it beats to propel itself through the water.

Adapted for Life in the Dark

The olm's underground streams and pools occur in the "karst" landscape that is associated with limestone. Living in permanent darkness, it has only tiny rudimentary eyes that are covered by skin. Its larvae, on the other hand, have quite well-developed eyes, but they degenerate during life. The adults lack dark pigment in their skin, but vary in color, being white, pink, gray, or yellowy; younger individuals often have darker blotches on the skin.

Unable to see, the olm must rely on other senses to find its food and for social communication. It has an excellent sense of smell, and its skin contains large numbers of tiny lateral line organs that are sensitive to water-borne vibrations. It uses its sense of smell and sensitivity to vibrations to detect the moving invertebrates on which it feeds. These senses are also important during aggressive interactions between males and during courtship and mating.

In 1994 a distinct form of the olm was discovered. Given the status of a subspecies, *Proteus anguinus parkelj* is black, has well-developed eyes, and is found only in the Bela Krajuna region of southeastern Slovenia. Individuals have been observed emerging from caves at night and swimming around in open pools and streams.

DATA PANEL

Olm (blind cave salamander)

Proteus anguinus

Family: Proteidae

World population: Unknown

Distribution: Southeastern Europe: the Adriatic coast from northern Italy to Montenegro (former Yugoslavia)

Habitat: Caves and underground lakes and streams in limestone mountains

Size: Length: 8–11 in (20–28 cm)

Form: Large, flat head with rounded snout; white, pale-gray, pink, or creamy-yellow elongated body; darker blotches in younger animals; large pink, feathery external gills. Small rudimentary limbs

Diet: Small aquatic invertebrates, mainly crustaceans

Breeding: Any time of year. Eggs fertilized internally. Twelve to 70 eggs laid under a stone and guarded by female until hatched; alternatively, just 1–2 eggs develop inside body of female, who gives birth to well-developed larvae. Young mature at 7 years. Life span up to 58 years

Related endangered species: None

Status: IUCN VU

Breeding

Living underground, the olm is not exposed to the seasonal variations in temperature and rainfall that are experienced by amphibians living on the surface. Water temperature in its cave habitat is more or less constant all year round. As a result, the olm has no obvious breeding season but may breed at any time of year. When breeding, the slightly smaller males become aggressive toward one another, defending their territory. If a female enters a male's territory, he performs a tail-fanning display—similar to that of European newts—in which he beats the tip of his tail rapidly against his flank. This creates a water current that he directs toward the female, who receives both vibratory stimuli and odor cues. If she is sexually responsive, she will approach the male. He then turns away, stopping to deposit a packet of sperm (called a spermatophore) on the ground. The female follows him and passes over the spermatophore. As she does so, her cloaca (cavity in the pelvic region into which the genital ducts open) passes over the spermatophore, and the sperm is drawn up into her body.

The female then creates a simple nest in the debris on the cave floor and lays a clutch of eggs. She guards them against predators until they hatch. Alternatively, between one and two eggs develop inside the body of the female, who gives birth to well-developed larvae.

Habitat at Risk

The olm's specialized habitat requirements—places where there are underground caves containing water—mean that even under ideal conditions it will always be a rare species.

Although it is reasonably safe from many of the changes that have adversely affected surface-living amphibians, such as habitat destruction, it is not wholly unaffected by events on the surface. Much of the water that fills the underground caves flows in from the surface, where it can become contaminated by a range of pollutants, such as agricultural runoff or industrial waste. It is believed that pollution is a major factor in the reduction of the olm population.

The olm is a fascinating animal, both to scientists and to amateur enthusiasts. In the past olms were collected as pig food. Today it is collection by enthusiasts that is having a more serious effect on natural populations.

The olm *lacks any dark pigment. Instead, individuals show a variety of pale colors, from pink to creamy yellow.*

Mallorcan Midwife Toad

Alytes muletensis

The Mallorcan midwife toad has an unusual reproductive strategy. Confined to a restricted habitat, it is now being sustained by a captive-breeding and release program.

The tiny Mallorcan midwife toad was known as a fossil long before it was discovered alive; it was found alive and named as recently as 1977. Now confined to about 10 isolated localities in the Sierra de Tramuntana, a mountainous region in western Mallorca, it once lived throughout the island. Its natural habitat is now fully protected, and a captive-breeding program is producing a steady supply of young animals that are released annually into suitable new sites.

Smaller than the three species of midwife toads that live on the European mainland, the Mallorcan midwife toad became isolated about 7 million years ago, when a rise in sea level separated Mallorca from Spain. Living in streams, pools, and wells throughout the island, its survival came under threat in Roman times, when nonnative animals were introduced to the island. The viperine snake is a predator of midwife toads, while the Spanish green frog is a competitor, its tadpoles feeding on the same kind of food. Both species thrive at low altitudes, but have not been able to colonize Mallorca's impressive mountainous regions. As a result, the Mallorcan midwife toad is confined to a few remote limestone ravines.

DATA PANEL

Mallorcan midwife toad (ferreret)

Alytes muletensis

Family: Discoglossidae

World population: 1,000–3,000 adults

Distribution: Mallorca

Habitat: Around pools in deep ravines at high altitude

Size: Length: 1.2–1.8 in (3–4 cm)

Form: Pale yellow or ocher with numerous dark-brown, black, or dark-green spots

Diet: Small invertebrates

Breeding: Spring and summer (March–July). Male carries eggs wrapped around hindlegs for several weeks; tadpole development lasts about 1 year

Related endangered species: Betic midwife toad *(Alytes dickhilleni)* VU

Status: IUCN VU

Call of the Wild

Following winter rains, which briefly turn their habitat into a raging torrent, Mallorcan midwife toads begin to call. The call is a soft, simple "peep" and, unusually, is produced by both sexes. It enables individuals to find each other in deep, rocky fissures. Mating, which takes place on land, is complex and protracted, and involves an elaborate series of leg movements by which a string of ten to 20 large, yolk-filled eggs becomes tightly wrapped around the male's hindlegs. The male then carries them around for several weeks until they are ready to hatch.

The brooding period lasts for three to 10 weeks and averages four weeks; it is longer in cold weather and can be costly for males. While carrying eggs, males are not able to pursue prey actively and so tend to lose weight. In addition, the egg string sometimes becomes so tightly wrapped around a leg that its blood supply is cut off and the leg is lost.

When the eggs are fully developed, the male briefly enters a pool and deposits them; soon afterward they hatch into tadpoles.

Tadpole development and growth can take more than a year, and the tadpoles grow to a considerable size. Indeed, growth in the tadpole stage represents a greater proportion of total lifetime growth than in any other frog.

Having passed a string of eggs to a male, the female, liberated from parental duties, develops a new batch of eggs; by the time they are mature, after about three weeks, there are males available who have gotten rid of their first batch of eggs. The breeding season lasts several months, and during it a female can lay up to three or four batches of eggs. Because females can generally produce eggs faster than males can brood them (an effect that is especially marked in cool weather), females commonly have to fight one another to mate with a willing male.

On the Brink of Extinction

When zoologists discovered the Mallorcan midwife toad alive, they realized that it was not only extremely rare, but also in danger of extinction. Its restricted habitat was a major cause for concern. It was immediately protected, and in 1985 a captive-breeding program was established involving a number of zoos and universities across Europe. The Mallorcan midwife toad thrives and breeds readily in captivity, and by 1989 large numbers of tadpoles and young adults were being shipped back to Mallorca to be released into the wild. Releases were made at localities with a suitable habitat where there were no wild toads. The species is now established at 12 new sites, in addition to the 13 natural ones. The range over which the species occurs has been doubled, and it is estimated that about 25 percent of the total population was bred in captivity. In 2004 its status was reduced from Critically Endangered to Vulnerable.

The Mallorcan midwife toad illustrates the potential of captive-breeding programs in the conservation of endangered animals. It is a particularly suitable technique for amphibians because they have a high reproductive potential that is only rarely realized under natural conditions. Amphibians typically produce a large number of eggs. However, most die, either as eggs or tadpoles, through a variety of natural causes in the wild. In captivity eggs and tadpoles can be protected from such hazards so that the reproductive potential of a species can be exploited.

The Mallorcan midwife toad *now provides a focal point for an environmental education program that involves other threatened species in Mallorca.*

EX
EW
CR
EN
VU
NT
LC
O

Golden Toad

Bufo periglenes

The golden toad has become a symbol of declining amphibian populations. Although living in a protected habitat, the species disappeared along with several other frog and toad species, and in 2004 was listed as extinct. The cause of this dramatic decline is unknown.

Most toads belonging to the genus *Bufo* are dull in color. Males and females are generally similar in appearance, with the females slightly larger than the males. The golden toad was highly unusual in that the coloration of the male was strikingly different from that of the female. While the female was greenish-yellow and black, decorated with yellow-edged red spots, the male was bright orange or red. The biological significance of the color difference is unknown.

Golden toads lived in "elfin" cloud forest, so called because the trees' growth is stunted by powerful winds. When the forest is shrouded in dense cloud, it creates a damp climate that favors the growth of epiphytic plants and creepers (plants that grow on other plants, but are not parasitic). The toads had been seen only in the breeding season from March to June following the rain and lasting only a few days or weeks. The rain fills small pools—many form around the roots of trees—that were essential for the breeding biology of the species. Large numbers of golden toads gathered at the shallow pools, with males typically outnumbering females.

Tadpole Survival

Most toads lay very large numbers of small eggs (several thousand in many species) that hatch into tiny tadpoles. The eggs of the golden toad, however, were large, with a sizeable part consisting of yolk, and the average clutch size was only about 300. It is thought that this pattern evolved because the breeding pools used by the golden toad could become very crowded and did not support a sufficient growth of algae to provide food for large numbers of tadpoles. Golden toad tadpoles needed the nutrients provided by the yolk if they were to grow quickly and metamorphose (transform into an adult) before their breeding ponds dried out.

BELIZE
HONDURAS
EL SALVADOR
NICARAGUA
COSTA RICA
PANAMA

The golden toad *appears to have been a victim of climate change. It has probably gone extinct because its habitat became too dry for breeding.*

DATA PANEL

Golden toad (sapo dorado)

Bufo periglenes

Family: Bufonidae

World population: Probably 0

Habitat: Montane (mountainous) cloud forest

Distribution: Monteverde Cloud Forest Preserve, Cordillera de Tilaran, Costa Rica

Size: Length: male 1.5–2 in (4.1–4.8 cm); female 1.8–2.3 in (4.7–5.4 cm)

Form: Male bright red or orange; female mottled black, red, and yellow

Diet: Insects and other invertebrates

Breeding: Clutch size of about 300 eggs laid March–June; hatch into tadpoles

Related endangered species: Amatola toad *(Bufo amatolicus)* CR; western toad *(B. boreas)* NT; Yosemite toad *(B. canorus)* EN; black toad *(B. exsul)* VU; Houston toad *(B. houstonensis)* EN; Amargosa toad *(B. nelsoni)* EN

Status: IUCN EX

Most toads lay their eggs in large, permanent ponds that are rich in algae and other nutrients.

Mysterious Decline

The golden toad was first described in 1964, having been observed during the breeding season. In 1987 1,500 animals were counted, but in both 1988 and 1989 only one individual was recorded at Monteverde in Costa Rica. Since then not a single golden toad has been seen. Over the same period about 20 percent of the frog and toad species found at Monteverde declined dramatically in numbers. During this time 25 species disappeared; only five have reappeared since. The species that were affected were those most dependent on standing water for breeding.

The cause of the dramatic population decline is not understood. Monteverde is a nature reserve and is not subject to habitat destruction of any kind, nor are any herbicides, pesticides, or other chemicals used in the locality.

A detailed analysis of the climate at Monteverde suggests that climate change may be responsible for the demise of the golden toad and other frog and toad species. Since the 1970s the number of days each year when the forest is shrouded in cloud has diminished, affecting the local fauna. Bird and reptile species that once occurred at lower, drier altitudes have moved into higher altitudes. It seems that the golden toads died out when their habitat became too dry for successful breeding.

EX
EW
CR
EN
VU
NT
LC
O

Western Toad

Bufo boreas

Once common throughout the western United States and Canada, the western toad has vanished from many parts of its range over the last 30 years. Although its decline is well documented, the causes of its depleted numbers are not known.

The huge geographical range of the western toad, stretching from the Baja California region of Mexico in the south to Alaska in the north; from sea level to altitudes of over 11,800 feet (3,600 m), suggests that it is a very adaptable species. It is found in a wide variety of habitats, including desert streams, grassland, woodland, and mountain meadows—its main requirement is only some kind of temporary or permanent water body nearby where it can breed. The western toad's remarkable ability to live in such a diversity of habitats has not, however, prevented it from declining and, in some areas, probably becoming extinct.

Gray or green in color with dark blotches, the western toad has a distinctive white or cream stripe running down the middle of its back. Its skin is warty, the warts mostly positioned within the dark blotches, some of which may be a rusty red color. Compared to many toads, it has rather small hind legs, and it typically runs over the ground, rather than hops. The male is, on average, slightly smaller than the female and somewhat less warty.

Two subspecies are recognized. The boreal toad occupies the northern part of the range, whereas the California toad is found farther south in California, western Nevada, and Baja California in Mexico.

DATA PANEL

Western toad (boreal toad)

Bufo boreas

Family: Bufonidae

World population: More than 100,000

Distribution: Western U.S. and Canada

Habitat: Varied: includes desert streams and springs, grassland, woodland, and mountain meadows; in or near ponds, lakes, reservoirs, rivers, and streams

Size: Length: 2.5–5 in (6.2–12.5 cm)

Form: Brown, gray, or greenish with large, dark blotches; often also some rusty-red blotches; white or cream stripe down the middle of the back; warty skin

Diet: Small invertebrates

Breeding: Spring and summer (January–July, depending on latitude, altitude, and local conditions); explosive breeder; female produces thousands of eggs in long strings

Related endangered species: Amargosa toad *(Bufo nelsoni)* EN; Amatola toad *(B. amatolicus)* CR; black toad *(B. exsul)* VU; Houston toad *(B. houstonensis)* EN; Yosemite toad *(B. canorus)* EN

Status: IUCN NT

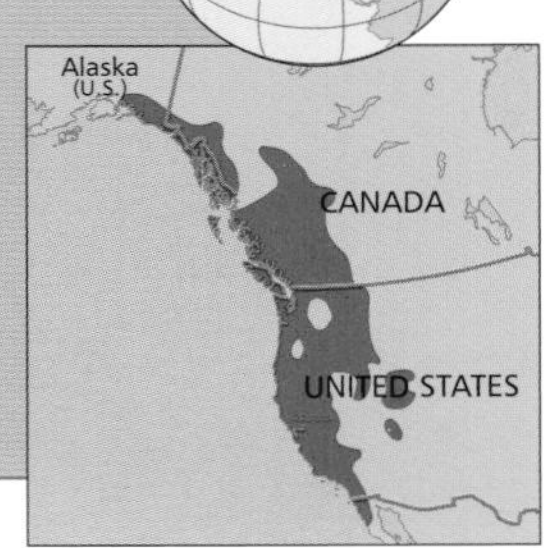

Explosive Breeding

The western toad spends much of its life underground, either digging into soft soil or using the burrows of other animals, such as ground squirrels. It is described as an "explosive breeder," meaning that it has a very short and frenetic breeding season. Early in the spring—which can be any time from late January to July, depending on latitude, altitude, and local climatic conditions—large numbers of toads suddenly emerge from their winter hiding places and move toward ponds, lakes, and streams. Males do not call to attract females, but simply move around a breeding pond looking for females. At lower altitudes western toads are generally active only during the night, but at higher altitudes where it is cold at night, they are active by day. In the water the more numerous males grapple over females. Once a pair is firmly clasped together, the male on the female's back, they make their way to a spawn site, where the female lays two long strings of eggs. Spawning is usually communal, with all the females in a population laying their eggs in one spot. The most likely benefit of such behavior is that the temperature inside a mass of spawn is slightly higher than that of the surrounding water, encouraging more rapid development of the eggs.

Population Decline

A survey carried out in Colorado in 1982 revealed that 11 populations of western toads known to exist in 1971 had vanished. In 1988 surveys in the central Rocky Mountains found western toads in only 10 of the 59 historically recorded sites. In Yosemite National Park in 1992 they were present in only one of many sites where they had been recorded in 1924. The species is now virtually extinct in Utah, and in Wyoming it has declined in the Yellowstone and Grand Teton National Parks.

Over much of its range the western toad has probably been adversely affected by deforestation, which has destroyed and fragmented its habitat. The period over which it has declined has also been a time when several serious droughts have occurred, preventing breeding in some years. Such factors do not explain the decline of the species in protected areas where its habitat has not been destroyed.

At some sites up to 95 percent of eggs have failed to hatch, a rate of mortality that is associated with an infection by the freshwater fungus, *Saprolegnia ferax*. The tendency of the species to breed communally exacerbates the effect of fungal infection. Experimental studies have shown that mortality among the eggs of western toads, as for other species, is increased by exposure to the elevated levels of ultraviolet radiation (especially UV-B) that now frequently occur in areas such as Oregon as a result of thinning of the ozone layer. Disease has also been suggested as a cause of the toad declines. Another possibility is that one or more environmental factors, such as increased UV-B or pollution, has weakened their immune systems so that they have lost their resistance to once-harmless diseases.

The western toad *is an adaptable species inhabiting a huge range throughout the western United States. It is found in a variety of habitats, from mountain meadows to deserts.*

EX
EW
CR
EN
VU
NT
LC
O

Golden Mantella

Mantella aurantiaca

The golden mantella frog is only found in one small forest on the island of Madagascar. It is threatened by the destruction of its habitat and by the international pet trade in frogs.

The golden mantella is one of a small group of frog species found only in Madagascar. It is brightly colored, poisonous, and active by day. It shares such characteristics with the poison-dart (dendrobatid) frogs of Central and South America. In evolutionary terms, however, the golden mantellas and poison-dart frogs are not related. The golden mantella thus represents an example of "convergent evolution" by which organisms come to closely resemble one another not as a result of common evolutionary ancestry, but through the action of natural selection (the survival of individuals best adjusted to their environment). The exact relationships of the mantellas are not clear. Some authorities put them in the large family Ranidae; others in a small family of their own: the Mantellidae.

Like the poison-dart frogs, the mantellas acquire poisonous compounds, called alkaloids, from their insect prey. They incorporate the toxic substances into secretions made in numerous poison glands in their skin. Predators that attack toxic, brightly colored prey quickly learn to associate the striking color pattern with an unpleasant experience and thereafter avoid that particular kind of prey.

Terrestrial Mating

Unlike many frogs, mantellas do not mate in standing water. However, they need damp conditions to breed and consequently mate in the rainy season. Males call to females, producing a sound like a cricket's chirp that consists of a series of notes, with three "clicks" in each. When a receptive female approaches, the male clasps her in a brief amplexus (mating embrace), during which the eggs are laid in hollows in the damp soil. There are suggestions that fertilization is internal, but mating has not been properly observed. The eggs are whitish in color, and there are between 20 and 75 in a clutch. They hatch after about 14 days; the tadpoles push their way up to the soil surface and then wriggle over the damp ground to a nearby pool. There they complete their development, emerging as tiny frogs about two months later. In contrast to the vivid adult coloration, newly metamorphosed golden mantellas are green and black.

A Race against Time

The golden mantella lives only in one small forest area between Beforona and Maramanga in western Madagascar. The forests of Madagascar have been largely destroyed. Trees have been felled over large areas to be exported as timber and to create land for agriculture. All kinds of animals that are unique to the island are threatened by such activity, and biologists are currently exploring the remaining forest fragments to catalog the endemic (native) fauna before it disappears. As a result of the intense exploration, a growing number of newly described Madagascan species, including mantellas, are emerging. A few years ago only three mantellas had been described, but the most recent analysis lists 12 species, all of which are listed by IUCN at some level of threat.

Mantellas are also threatened by international trade, being popular as pets in Europe, the United States, and elsewhere. Since they are small and mainly terrestrial, the frogs are relatively easy to keep in captivity. In addition, they can be induced to breed, a factor that may be crucial for their conservation. All species are listed under CITES.

DATA PANEL

Golden mantella

Mantella aurantiaca

Family: Ranidae/Mantellidae

World population: Unknown

Distribution: Eastern Madagascar

Habitat: Deep leaf litter in wet tropical forests

Size: Length: 0.8–1.3 in (2–3 cm)

Form: Adults bright yellow, orange, or red; newly metamorphosed frogs green and black; black eyes

Diet: Small invertebrates

Breeding: Clutch of 20–75 whitish eggs laid in dark cavities on land; eggs hatch after about 14 days; tadpoles wriggle to small pools and emerge as tiny frogs about 2 months later

Related endangered species: 11 other mantellas listed by IUCN as threatened

Status: IUCN CR

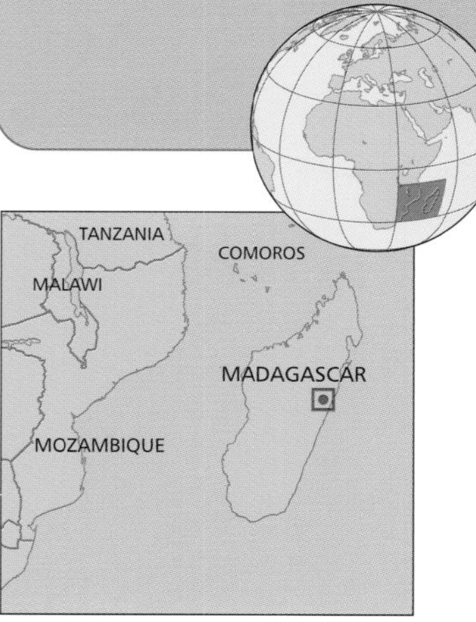

Adult golden mantellas *are both vividly colored and poisonous, a combination known as aposematic or warning coloration.*

EX
EW
CR
EN
VU
NT
LC
O

Tomato Frog

Dyscophus antongilii

The red or orange-colored tomato frog of Madagascar has been threatened by habitat destruction, pollution, and overcollection for the pet trade. It is now protected and responding well to captive-breeding programs.

The tomato frog gets its name from the rounded shape of the female and her red coloration, which makes her resemble a ripe tomato. Not all tomato frogs are red; some are orange, others dark brown, and males are generally less vividly colored than females. The frog has a flat head, a rounded body, and white underside; females are considerably larger than males. Their striking coloration, combined with the fact that they thrive in captivity, have made them popular animals in the international pet trade.

Found only in Madagascar, the tomato frog has a small range. It occurs in two main areas on the coastal plain in the northeast of the island. Its preferred habitat is soft soil, where standing water for it to breed in accumulates during the rainy season. A secretive, nocturnal animal, it hides during the day, emerging at night to hunt ground-dwelling invertebrates. The frog's round shape and lack of adhesive disks on its fingers and toes mean that it is unable to climb. Nor is it particularly well adapted for swimming, having only partial webbing between its toes and none between its fingers. During the dry season it burrows deep into sandy soil, using horny protuberances on its hind feet.

DATA PANEL

Tomato frog

Dyscophus antongilii

Family: Microhylidae

World population: Unknown

Distribution: Eastern coastal plains of Madagascar

Habitat: Lowland habitats with soft soil; some agricultural areas

Size: Length: male 2.5 in (6.5 cm); female 3.3–4.8 in (8–12 cm)

Form: Flat head, plump body, partial webbing between toes. Female bright red, occasionally orange or dark brown on the back; belly white. Male has duller, yellow-orange coloration

Diet: Small invertebrates

Breeding: 1,000–1,500 black-and-white eggs laid on water surface; tadpoles hatch within 36 hours; metamorphosis complete at 6.5 weeks; fully mature at 12 months. Life span 10 years

Related endangered species: Neither of the 2 other known species of *Dyscophus* is threatened

Status: IUCN NT

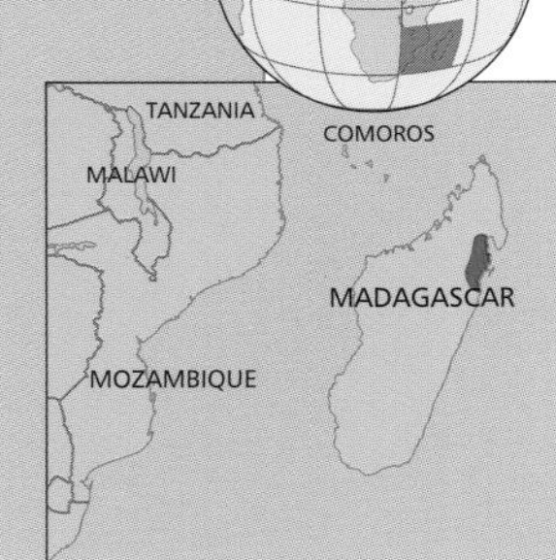

Sticky Defense

In many amphibians bright coloration is associated with skin toxins that make them unpalatable or poisonous to potential predators. The tomato frog's bright color serves to warn predators that it is not good to eat. When attacked or handled, it secretes copious amounts of sticky mucus from its skin; any animal trying to eat it is likely to find its jaws glued together. A number of amphibians have this kind of defense, but the tomato frog produces mucus with stronger sticking power than that of any other frog. It is also mildly toxic, often causing an allergic reaction in humans.

Breeding after Rain

With the first indication of rain male tomato frogs emerge from underground and head for ditches, ponds, and pools as they fill with water. It is thought that the sound of rain falling on the ground is a sufficient stimulus to bring males out of hiding. Males call to attract females from the edge of the water, inflating a single vocal patch under the chin. Females lay between 1,000 and 1,500 eggs that float on the surface of the water. Filter-feeding tadpoles hatch from the eggs within two days and take a further six weeks to metamorphose into juvenile froglets. The young frogs are about 0.4 inches (1 cm) long by this stage and black or brown with a tan stripe down the back. They develop the characteristic adult colors at about three months and are fully mature by one year.

Threats and Conservation

The tomato frog has a restricted range in Madagascar, and much of its natural habitat has been destroyed to make way for building and agricultural land. This has not been as disastrous for the tomato frog as for other species, since they thrive alongside human activities and habitations. Large breeding populations form in human-made drainage ditches, rice fields, and flooded meadows, but these habitats are susceptible to pollution from pesticides, herbicides, and detergents.

The main threat to the tomato frog comes from the worldwide trade in amphibians. Large numbers used to be exported from Madagascar to Europe and the United States. Although it is nocturnal, the frog's distinctive nighttime call made it possible for poachers to identify and capture it in the dark.

The trade in tomato frogs for pets has now been stopped. The species is fully protected under CITES and breeding successfully in captivity, although lack of genetic diversity is a problem. To help increase diversity, attempts will be made to crossbreed frogs from European and American collections. The aim is also to build up captive populations in Madagascar for export to foreign breeding programs. The pet-trade market could then be met by captive-bred, rather than wild-caught frogs, and captive-bred animals could be used to reestablish populations in the wild.

The female tomato frog's *vivid red color has made it a target of poachers in its native Madagascar. CITES legislation has now outlawed this practice.*

Gastric-brooding Frog

Rheobatrachus silus

Notable for the unique mode of reproduction by which they are named, the gastric-brooding frogs of Queensland were never common. They may have been wiped out by a disease that has affected many frogs in Australia.

With the extinction of its two species of gastric-brooding frog, Australia—and the world—have lost animals with a unique form of reproduction. Found only in a small area of Queensland, the gastric-brooding frog was not discovered until 1973. It has not been seen in the wild since 1981, despite several intensive searches being made. The decline in its population was particularly dramatic during 1979. The last laboratory specimen died in 1983. The frog's close relative, the northern gastric-brooding frog, which was not discovered until 1984, also suffered a catastrophic population decline in the following year and is now also extinct.

Little is known about the gastric-brooding frog's behavior; mating has never been observed, for example. However, its breeding patterns are unique.

DATA PANEL

Gastric-brooding frog (platypus frog)

Rheobatrachus silus

Family: Myobatrachidae

World population: Extinct

Distribution: Southeastern Queensland, Australia

Habitat: Rocky mountain creeks

Size: Length: male 1.3–1.6 in (3.3–4.1 cm); female 1.8–2.2 in (4.5–5.4 cm)

Form: Small frog with blunt snout, large eyes, long fingers and toes, and webbed hind feet. Brown or black on back; white on belly; yellow on limbs

Diet: Small invertebrates

Breeding: In summer (November to January) female lays 26–40 eggs and swallows them; they develop inside her stomach; 6–25 froglets are delivered through the mouth after a gestation period of 6–7 weeks

Related endangered species: Southern gastric-brooding frog *(Rheobatrachus vitellinus)* EX

Status: IUCN EX

Most species of frog lay eggs in water or on moist ground, or they develop inside one of the parents. Fertilization is mostly external, and the eggs generally pass through a free-swimming tadpole stage. Sometimes, however, the tadpoles are immobile and develop directly into tiny froglets. In the gastric-brooding frog females are known to lay between 26 and 40 eggs. However, at some stage in their development, either as eggs or as tadpoles, the female swallows some or all of her offspring, which then develop in her stomach. The process of swallowing the young has never been seen. After six or seven weeks the female delivers between six and 25 fully developed but tiny froglets through her mouth.

Some aspects of the frog's extraordinary reproductive system were studied in the laboratory by a scientist called Michael Tyler. He reasoned that for the mode of reproduction to work, there must be a mechanism by which the young are not digested by their mother's gastric juices. Tyler found that the developing larvae secrete prostaglandin, a hormonelike chemical that inhibits (prevents) the production of digestive acid by the mother's stomach. The chemical is also thought to inhibit peristalsis—the involuntary muscular contractions that move food along the alimentary tract during digestion.

Hidden Habitat

Confined to the Conondale and Blackall mountain ranges in southeastern Queensland, the gastric-brooding frog is well adapted to its aquatic way of life. The toes of the hind feet are fully webbed, enabling it to swim powerfully, and it has upward-pointing eyes that help it see above the waterline.

The gastric-brooding frog's preferred habitat is rocky mountain creeks, where it spends most of the day hiding under rocks. It leaves the water to feed, going in search of live prey. Unlike many frogs, it does not have a protrusible tongue (one that can be pushed out), but catches its prey by lunging at it with an open mouth. During the breeding season males call females from the water's edge.

The slightly larger northern gastric-brooding frog lived in a similar habitat and also had a very restricted range, in the Clarke Mountains near Mackay in central coastal Queensland.

Mysterious Decline

The two gastric-brooding frogs are among several species that declined in high-altitude habitats in Queensland. The declines are puzzling because they have occurred in protected areas where the forest has been conserved.

It is now thought that the declines are a result of a disease that has spread rapidly in Queensland as well as other parts of Australia and Central America. The disease is called chytridiomycosis and is caused by a microscopic organism called a chytrid fungus.

The fungus is a parasite that invades the skin of amphibians, where it reproduces, digesting keratin, the fibrous protein in the outer layer of the skin. The tadpoles of frogs do not have keratin in their skin, except in the horny beak around their mouth, so they can carry the chytrid fungus without being adversely affected by it.

How the chytrid fungus kills frogs is not yet understood. One possibility is that it interferes with the passage of water and oxygen across a frog's skin; another is that it produces a substance that is toxic to frogs. It is not yet known how the disease found its way to Australia, although the most likely route was through amphibians introduced into the locality from elsewhere in the world.

The gastric-brooding frog *had prominent, upward-pointing eyes, enabling it to see above the waterline.*

Categories of Threat

The status categories that appear in the data panel for each species throughout this book are based on those published by the International Union for the Conservation of Nature (IUCN). They provide a useful guide to the current status of the species in the wild, and governments throughout the world use them when assessing conservation priorities and in policy-making. However, they do not provide automatic legal protection for the species.

Animals are placed in the appropriate category after scientific research. More species are being added all the time, and animals can be moved from one category to another as their circumstances change.

Extinct (EX)

A group of animals is classified as EX when there is no reasonable doubt that the last individual has died.

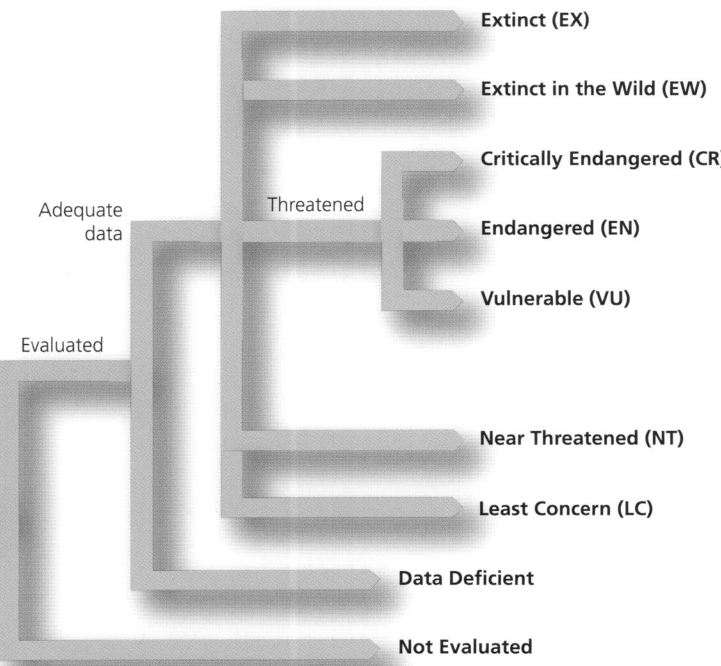

Extinct in the Wild (EW)

Animals in this category are known to survive only in captivity or as a population established artificially by introduction somewhere well outside its former range. A species is categorized as EW when exhaustive surveys throughout the areas where it used to occur consistently fail to record a single individual. It is important that such searches be carried out over all of the available habitat and during a season or time of day when the animals should be present.

Critically Endangered (CR)

The category CR includes animals facing an extremely high risk of extinction in the wild in the immediate future. It includes any of the following:

- Any species with fewer than 50 individuals, even if the population is stable.
- Any species with fewer than 250 individuals if the population is declining, badly fragmented, or all in one vulnerable group.
- Animals from larger populations that have declined by 80 percent within 10 years (or are predicted to do so) or three generations, whichever is the longer.

The IUCN categories *of threat. The system displayed has operated for new and reviewed assessments since January 2001.*

• Species living in a very small area—defined as under 39 square miles (100 sq. km).

Endangered (EN)

A species is EN when it is not CR but is nevertheless facing a very high risk of extinction in the wild in the near future. It includes any of the following:

• A species with fewer than 250 individuals remaining, even if the population is stable.

• Any species with fewer than 2,500 individuals if the population is declining, badly fragmented, or all in one vulnerable subpopulation.

• A species whose population is known or expected to decline by 50 percent within 10 years or three generations, whichever is the longer.

• A species whose range is under 1,900 square miles (5,000 sq. km), and whose range, numbers, or population levels are declining, fragmented, or fluctuating wildly.

• Species for which there is a more than 20 percent likelihood of extinction in the next 20 years or five generations, whichever is the longer.

Vulnerable (VU)

A species is VU when it is not CR or EN but is facing a high risk of extinction in the wild in the medium-term future. It includes any of the following:

• A species with fewer than 1,000 mature individuals remaining, even if the population is stable.

• Any species with fewer than 10,000 individuals if the population is declining, badly fragmented, or all in one vulnerable subpopulation.

• A species whose population is known, believed, or expected to decline by 20 percent within 10 years or

The Komodo *National Park (left) was created in 1980 to help maintain Komodo dragon populations on the Indonesian islands of Komodo, Rinca, and Padar.*

three generations, whichever is the longer.

- A species whose range is less than 772 square miles (20,000 sq. km), and whose range, numbers, or population structure are declining, fragmented, or fluctuating wildly.
- Species for which there is a more than 10 percent likelihood of extinction in the next 100 years.

Near Threatened/Least Concern (since 2001)

In January 2001 the classification of lower-risk species was changed. Near Threatened (NT) and Least Concern (LC) were introduced as separate categories. They replaced the previous Lower Risk (LR) category with its subdivisions of Conservation Dependent (LRcd), Near Threatened (LRnt), and Least Concern (LRlc). From January 2001 all new assessments and reassessments must adopt NT or LC if relevant. But the older categories still apply to some animals until they are reassessed, and will also be found in this book.

- Near Threatened (NT)

Animals that do not qualify for CR, EN, or VU categories now but are close to qualifying or are likely to qualify for a threatened category in the future.

- Least Concern (LC)

Animals that have been evaluated and do not qualify for CR, EN, VU, or NT categories.

Lower Risk (before 2001)

- Conservation Dependent (LRcd)

Animals whose survival depends on an existing conservation program

- Near Threatened (LRnt)

Animals for which there is no conservation program but that are close to qualifying for VU category.

- Least Concern (LRlc)

Species that are not conservation dependent or near threatened.

By monitoring *populations of threatened animals like this American rosy boa, biologists help keep the IUCN Red List up to date.*

Scientists hope *that diminishing wild populations of tomato frogs will be replenished when captive-breeding programs are successful.*

Data Deficient (DD)

A species or population is DD when there is not enough information on abundance and distribution to assess the risk of extinction. In some cases, when the species is thought to live only in a small area, or a considerable period of time has passed since the species was last recorded, it may be placed in a threatened category as a precaution.

Not Evaluated (NE)

Such animals have not yet been assessed.

Note: a colored panel in each entry in this book indicates the current level of threat to the species. The two new categories (NT and LC) and two of the earlier Lower Risk categories (LRcd and LRnt) are included within the band LR; the old LRlc is included along with Data Deficient (DD) and Not Evaluated (NE) under "Other," abbreviated to "O."

CITES *lists animals in the major groups in three Appendices, depending on the level of threat posed by international trade.*

	Appendix I	Appendix II	Appendix III
Mammals	277 species 16 subspecies 14 populations	295 species 12 subspecies 12 populations	45 species 8 subspecies
Birds	152 species 11 subspecies 2 populations	1,268 species 6 subspecies 1 populations	35 species
Reptiles	75 species 5 subspecies 6 populations	527 species 4 subspecies 4 populations	55 species
Amphibians	16 species	98 species	
Fish	15 species	71 species	
Invertebrates	62 species 4 subspecies	2,100 species 1 subspecies	17 species

CITES APPENDICES

Appendix I lists the most endangered of traded species, namely those that are threatened with extinction and will be harmed by continued trade. These species are usually protected in their native countries and can only be imported or exported with a special permit. Permits are required to cover the whole transaction—both exporter and importer must prove that there is a compelling scientific justification for moving the animal from one country to another. This includes transferring animals between zoos for breeding purposes. Permits are only issued when it can be proved that the animal was legally acquired and that the remaining population will not be harmed by the loss.

Appendix II includes species that are not currently threatened with extinction, but that could easily become so if trade is not carefully controlled. Some common animals are listed here if they resemble endangered species so closely that criminals could try to sell the rare species pretending they were a similar common one. Permits are required to export such animals, with requirements similar to those Appendix I species.

Appendix III species are those that are at risk or protected in at least one country. Other nations may be allowed to trade in animals or products, but they may need to prove that they come from safe populations.

CITES designations are not always the same for every country. In some cases individual countries can apply for special permission to trade in a listed species. For example, they might have a safe population of an animal that is very rare elsewhere. Some African countries periodically apply for permission to export large quantities of elephant tusks that have been in storage for years, or that are the product of a legal cull of elephants. This is controversial because it creates an opportunity for criminals to dispose of black market ivory by passing it off as coming from one of those countries where elephant products are allowed to be exported. If you look up the African elephant, you will see that it is listed as CITES I, II, and III, depending on the country location of the different populations.

Organizations

The human race is undoubtedly nature's worst enemy, but we can also help limit the damage caused by the rapid increase in our numbers and activities. There have always been people eager to protect the world's beautiful places and to preserve its most special animals, but it is only quite recently that the conservation message has begun to have a real effect on everyday life, government policy, industry, and agriculture.

Early conservationists were concerned with preserving nature for the benefit of people. They acted with an instinctive sense of what was good for nature and people, arguing for the preservation of wilderness and animals in the same way as others argued for the conservation of historic buildings or gardens. The study of ecology and environmental science did not really take off until the mid-20th century, and it took a long time for the true scale of our effect in the natural world to become apparent. Today the conservation of wildlife is based on far greater scientific understanding, but the situation has become much more complex and urgent in the face of human development.

By the mid-20th century extinction was becoming an immediate threat. Animals such as the passenger pigeon, quagga, and thylacine had disappeared despite last-minute attempts to save them. More and more species were discovered to be at risk, and species-focused conservation groups began to appear. In the early days there was little that any of these organizations could do but campaign against direct killing. Later they became a kind of conservation emergency service—rushing to the aid of seriously threatened animals in an attempt to save the species. But as time went on, broader environmental issues began to receive the urgent attention they needed. Research showed time and time again that saving species almost always comes down to addressing the problem of habitat loss. The world is short of space, and ensuring that there is enough for all the species is very difficult.

Conservation *organizations range from government departments in charge of national parks, such as Yellowstone National Park (right), the oldest in the United States, to local initiatives set up to protect endangered birds. Here (above) a man in Peru climbs a tree to check on the nest of a harpy eagle discovered near his village.*

Conservation is not just about animals and plants, nor even the protection of whole ecological systems. Conservation issues are so broad that they touch almost every aspect of our lives, and successful measures often depend on the expertise of biologists, ecologists, economists, diplomats, lawyers, social scientists, and businesspeople. Conservation is all about cooperation and teamwork. Often it is also about helping people benefit from taking care of their wildlife. The organizations involved vary from small groups of a few dozen enthusiasts in local communities to vast, multinational operations.

THE IUCN

With so much activity based in different countries, it is important to have a worldwide overview, some way of coordinating what goes on in different parts of the planet. That is the role of the International Union for the Conservation of Nature (IUCN), also referred to as the World Conservation Union. It began life as the International Union for the Preservation of Nature in 1948, becoming the IUCN in 1956. It is relatively new compared to the Sierra Club, Flora and Fauna International, and the Royal Society for the Protection of Birds. It was remarkable in that its founder members included governments, government agencies, and nongovernmental organizations. In the years following the appalling destruction of World War II, the IUCN was born out of a desire to draw a line under the horrors of the past and to act together to safeguard the future.

The mission of the IUCN is to influence, encourage, and assist societies throughout the world to conserve the diversity of nature and natural systems. It seeks to ensure that the use of natural resources is fair and ecologically sustainable. Based in Switzerland, the IUCN has over 1,000 permanent staff and the help of 11,000 volunteer experts from about 180 countries. The work of the IUCN is split into six commissions, which deal with protected areas, policy-making, ecosystem management, education, environmental law, and species survival. The Species Survival Commission (SSC) has almost 7,000 members, all experts in the study of plants and animals. Within the SSC there are Specialist Groups concerned with the conservation of different types of animals, from cats to flamingos, deer, ducks, bats, and crocodiles. Some particularly well-studied animals, such as the African elephant and the polar bear, have their own specialist groups.

Perhaps the best-known role of the IUCN SSC is in the production of the Red Data Books, or Red Lists. First published in 1966, the books were designed to be easily updated, with details of each species on a different page that could be removed and replaced as new information came to light.

By 2010 the Red Lists include information on about 45,000 types of animal, of which almost 10,000 are threatened with extinction. Gathering this amount of information together is a

The IUCN Red Lists *of threatened species are published online and can be accessed at:* ***http://www. iucnredlist.org***

huge task, but it provides an invaluable conservation resource. The Red Lists are continually updated and are now available on the World Wide Web. The Red Lists are the basis for the categories of threat used in this book.

CITES

CITES is the Convention on International Trade in Endangered Species of Wild Fauna and Flora (also known as the Washington Convention, since it first came into force after an international meeting in Washington D.C. in 1973). Currently 175 nations have agreed to implement the CITES regulations. Exceptions to the convention include Iraq and North Korea, which, for the time being at least, have few trading links with the rest of the world. Trading in animals and their body parts has been a major factor in the decline of some of the world's rarest species. The IUCN categories draw attention to the status of rare species, but they do not confer any legal protection. That is done through national laws.

Conventions serve as international laws. In the case of CITES, lists (called Appendices) are agreed on internationally and reviewed every few years. The Appendices list the species that are threatened by international trade. Animals are assigned to Appendix I when all trade is forbidden. Any specimens of these species, alive or dead (or skins, feathers, etc.), will be confiscated by customs at international borders, seaports, or airports. Appendix II species can be traded internationally, but only under strict controls. Wildlife trade is often valuable in the rural economy, and this raises difficult questions about the relative importance of animals and people. Nevertheless, traders who ignore CITES rules risk heavy fines or imprisonment. Some rare species—even those with the highest IUCN categories (many bats and frogs, for example)—may have no CITES protection simply because they have no commercial value. Trade is then not really a threat.

The Greenpeace ship, *seen here in Antarctica, travels to areas of conservation concern and helps draw worldwide media attention to environmental issues.*

WILDLIFE CONSERVATION ORGANIZATIONS

BirdLife International
BirdLife International is a partnership of 60 organizations working in more than 100 countries. Most partners are national nongovernmental conservation groups such as the Canadian Nature Federation. Others include large bird charities such as the Royal Society for the Protection of Birds in Britain. By working together within BirdLife International, even small organizations can be effective globally as well as on a local scale. BirdLife International is a member of the IUCN.
Web site: http://www.birdlife.org

Conservation International (CI)
Founded in 1987, Conservation International works closely with the IUCN and has a similar multinational approach. CI offers help in the world's most threatened biodiversity hot spots.
Web site: http://conservation.org

Durrell Wildlife Conservation Trust (DWCT)
Another IUCN member, the Durrell Wildlife Conservation Trust was founded by the British naturalist and author Gerald Durrell in 1963. The trust is based at Durrell's world-famous zoo on Jersey in the Channel Islands. Jersey was the world's first zoo dedicated solely to the conservation of endangered species. Breeding programs at the zoo have helped stabilize populations of some of the world's most endangered animals. The trust trains conservationists from many countries and works to secure areas of natural habitat to which animals can be returned. Jersey Zoo and the DWCT were instrumental in saving numerous species from extinction, including the pink pigeon, Mauritius kestrel, Waldrapp ibis, St. Lucia parrot, and the Telfair's skink and other reptiles.
Web site: http://durrell.org

Fauna & Flora International (FFI)
Founded in 1903, this organization has had various name changes. It began life as a society for protecting large mammals, but has broadened its scope. It was involved in saving the Arabian oryx from extinction.
Web site: http://www.fauna-flora.org

National Audubon Society
John James Audubon was an American naturalist and wildlife artist who died in 1851, 35 years before the society that bears his name was founded. The first Audubon Society was established by George Bird Grinnell in protest against the appalling overkill of birds for meat, feathers, and sport. By the end of the 19th century there were Audubon Societies in 15 states, and they later became part of the National Audubon Society, which funds scientific research programs, publishes

WILDLIFE CONSERVATION ORGANIZATIONS

magazines and journals, manages wildlife sanctuaries, and advises state and federal governments on conservation issues.
Web site: http://www.audubon.org

Pressure Groups
Friends of the Earth, founded in Britain in 1969, and Greenpeace, founded in 1971 in British Columbia, were the first environmental pressure groups to become internationally recognized. Greenpeace became known for "direct, nonviolent actions," which drew attention to major conservation issues. (For example, campaigners steered boats between the harpoon guns of whalers and their prey.)

The organizations offer advice to governments and corporations, and help those that seek to protect the environment, while continuing to name, shame, and campaign against those who do not.

Royal Society for the Protection of Birds
This organization was founded in the 1890s to campaign against the slaughter of birds to supply feathers for the fashion trade. It now has a wider role and has become Britain's premier wildlife conservation organization, with over a million members. It is involved in international activities, particularly in the protection of birds that migrate to Britain.
Web site: http://www.rspb.org.uk

The Sierra Club
The Sierra Club was started in 1892 by John Muir and is still going strong. Muir, a Scotsman by birth, is often thought of as the founder of the conservation movement, especially in the United States, where he campaigned for the preservation of wilderness. It was through his efforts that the first national parks, including Yosemite, Sequoia, and Mount Rainier, were established. Today the Sierra Club remains dedicated to the preservation of wild places for the benefit of wildlife and the enjoyment of people.
Web site: http://www.sierraclub.org

World Wide Fund for Nature (WWF)
The World Wide Fund for Nature, formerly the World Wildlife Fund, was born in 1961.
It was a joint venture between the IUCN, several existing conservation organizations, and a number of successful businesspeople. Unlike many charities, WWF was big, well-funded, and high profile from the beginning.
Its familiar giant panda emblem ranks alongside those of the Red Cross, Mercedes Benz, or Coca-Cola in terms of instant international recognition.
Web site: http://www.wwf.org

GLOSSARY

adaptation Features of an animal that adjust it to its environment; may be produced by evolution—e.g., camouflage coloration

adaptive radiation Where a group of closely related animals (e.g., members of a family) have evolved differences from each other so that they can survive in different niches

adhesive disks Flattened disks on the tips of the fingers or toes of certain climbing amphibians that enable them to cling to smooth, vertical surfaces

adult A fully grown sexually mature animal

amphibian Any cold-blooded vertebrate of the class Amphibia, typically living on land but breathing in the water; e.g., frogs, toads, newts, salamanders

amphibious Able to live on both land and in water

anterior The front part of an animal

biodiversity The variety of species and the variation within them

biome A major world landscape characterized by having similar plants and animals living in it, e.g., desert, rain forest, forest

carapace The upper part of a shell in a chelonian

carrion Rotting flesh of dead animals

casque The raised portion on the head of certain reptiles and birds

chelonian Any reptile of the order Chelonia, including the tortoises and turtles, in which most of the body is enclosed in a bony capsule

cloaca Cavity in the pelvic region into which the alimentary canal, genital, and urinary ducts open

costal grooves Grooves running around the body of some terrestrial salamanders; they conduct water from the ground to the upper parts of the body

deciduous forest Dominated by trees that lose their leaves in winter (or in the dry season)

deforestation The process of cutting down and removing trees for timber or to create open space for growing crops, grazing animals, etc.

diurnal Active during the day

DNA (deoxyribonucleic acid) The substance that makes up the main part of the chromosomes of all living things; contains the genetic code that is handed down from generation to generation

dorsal Relating to the back or spinal part of the body; usually the upper surface

ecology The study of plants and animals in relation to one another and to their surroundings

ecosystem A whole system in which plants, animals, and their environment interact

ectotherm Animal that relies on external heat sources to raise body temperature; also known as "cold-blooded"

endemic Found only in one geographical area, nowhere else

estivation Inactivity or greatly decreased activity during hot weather

eutrophication An increase in the nutrient chemicals (nitrate, phosphate, etc.) in water, sometimes occurring naturally and sometimes caused by human activities, e.g., by the release of sewage or agricultural fertilizers

explosive breeding In some amphibians when breeding is completed over one or a very few days and nights

extinction Process of dying out at the end of which the very last individual dies, and the species is lost forever

gene The basic unit of heredity, enabling one generation to pass on characteristics to its offspring

genus (genera, pl.) A group of closely related species

gill Respiratory organ that absorbs oxygen from the water. External gills occur in tadpoles. Internal gills occur in most fish

herbivore An animal that eats plants (grazers and browsers are herbivores)

herpetologist Zoologist who studies reptiles and amphibians

hibernation Becoming inactive in winter, with lowered body temperature to save energy. Hibernation takes place in a special nest or den called a hibernaculum

incubation The act of keeping the eggs warm or the period from laying the eggs to hatching

juvenile A young animal that has not yet reached breeding age

keel A ridge along the carapace of certain turtles or a ridge on the scales of some reptiles

keratin Tough, fibrous material that forms hair, feathers, nails, and protective plates on the skin of vertebrate animals

larva An immature form of an animal that develops into an adult form through metamorphosis

lateral line system A system of pores running along the body of some amphibians. These pores lead to nerve endings that allow the animal to sense vibrations in the water and help it locate prey, detect predators, avoid obstacles, and so on

livebearer Animal that gives birth to fully developed young (usually refers to reptiles or fish)

metabolic rate The rate at which chemical activities occur within animals, including the exchange of gasses in respiration and the liberation of energy from food

metamorphosis The transformation of a larva into an adult

osteoderms Bony plates beneath the scales of some reptiles, particularly crocodilians

oviparous Producing eggs that hatch outside the body of the mother (in fish, reptiles, birds, and monotremes)

plastron The lower shell of chelonians

posterior The hind end or behind another structure

prehensile Capable of grasping

reptile Any member of the cold-blooded class Reptilia, such as crocodiles, lizards, snakes, tortoises, turtles, and tuataras; characterized by an external covering of scales or horny plates. Most are egg-layers, but some give birth to fully developed young

scute Horny plate covering live body tissue underneath

spawning The laying and fertilizing of eggs by fish and amphibians and some mollusks

speciation The origin of species; the diverging of two similar organisms through reproduction down through the generations into different forms resulting in a new species

ventral Of or relating to the front part or belly of an animal (see dorsal)

vertebrate Animal with a backbone (e.g., fish, mammal, reptile), usually with skeleton made of bones, but sometimes softer cartilage

vestigial A characteristic with little or no use, but derived from one that was well developed in an ancestral form; e.g., the "parson's nose" (the fatty end portion of the tail when a fowl is cooked) is the compressed bones from the long tail of the reptilian ancestor of birds

viviparous (of most mammals and a few reptiles) Giving birth to active young rather than laying eggs

FURTHER RESEARCH

Books

Reptiles and Amphibians

Corbett, Keith, *Conservation of European Reptiles and Amphibians,* Christopher Helm, London, U.K., 1989

Corton, Misty, *Leopard and Other South African Tortoises,* Carapace Press, London, U.K., 2000

Hofrichter, Robert, *Amphibians: The World of Frogs, Toads, Salamanders, and Newts*, Firefly Books, Canada, 2000

Murphy, J. B., Adler, K., and Collins, J. T. (eds.), *Captive Management and Conservation of Reptiles and Amphibians*, Society for the Study of Amphibians and Reptiles, Ithaca, New York, 1994

Stafford, Peter, *Snakes*, Natural History Museum, London, U.K., 2000

Mammals

Macdonald, David, *The New Encyclopedia of Mammals,* Oxford University Press, Oxford, U.K., 2009

Payne, Roger, *Among Whales*, Bantam Press, U.S., 1996

Reeves, R. R., and Leatherwood, S., *The Sierra Club Handbook of Whales and Dolphins of the World*, Sierra Club, U.S., 1983

Sherrow, Victoria, and Cohen, Sandee, *Endangered Mammals of North America*, Twenty-First Century Books, U.S., 1995

Whitaker, J. O., Audubon Society *Field Guide to North American Mammals,* Alfred A. Knopf, New York, U.S., 1996

Wilson, Don E., Mittermeier, Russell A., *Handbook of Mammals of the World Vol 1,* Lynx Edicions, Barcelona, Spain, 2009

Birds

Attenborough, David, *The Life of Birds,* BBC Books, London, U.K., 1998

BirdLife International, *Threatened Birds of the World*, Lynx Edicions, Barcelona, Spain and BirdLife International, Cambridge, U.K., 2000

del Hoyo, J., Elliott, A., and Sargatal, J., eds., *Handbook of Birds of the World Vols 1 to 15,* Lynx Edicions, Barcelona, Spain, 1992–2010

Dunn, Jon, and Alderfer, Jonathan K., *National Geographic Field Guide to the Birds of North America,* National Geographic Society, Washington D.C., United States, 2006.

Stattersfield, A., Crosby, M., Long, A., and Wege, D., eds., *Endemic Bird Areas of the World: Priorities for Biodiversity Conservation,* BirdLife International, Cambridge, U.K., 1998

Fish

Buttfield, Helen, *The Secret Lives of Fishes*, Abrams, U.S., 2000

Dawes, John, and Campbell, Andrew, eds., *The New Encyclopedia of Aquatic Life, Facts On File*, New York, U.S., 2004

Insects

Eaton, Eric R. and Kaufman, Kenn. *Kaufman Field Guide to Insects of North America*, Houghton Mifflin, New York, U.S., 2007

Pyle, Robert Michael, National Audubon Society *Field Guide to North American Butterflies*, Pyle, Robert Michael, A. Knopf, New York, U.S., 1995

General

Allaby, Michael, *A Dictionary of Ecology*, Oxford University Press, New York, U.S., 2010

Douglas, Dougal, and others, *Atlas of Life on Earth*, Barnes & Noble, New York, U.S., 2001

Web sites

http://www.nature.nps.gov/ U.S. National Park Service wildlife site

http://www.ummz.lsa.umich-edu/ umich.edu/ University of Michigan Museum of Zoology animal diversity web. Search for pictures and information about animals by class, family, and common name

http://www.cites.org/ CITES and IUCN listings. Search for animals by order, family, genus, species, or common name. Location by country and explanation of reasons for listings

http://www.cmc-ocean.org Facts, figures, and quizzes about marine life

www.darwinfoundation.org/ Charles Darwin Research Center

http://www.amphibiaweb.org/ AmphibiaWeb. Information about amphibians and their conservation

http://www.fws.gov.endangered Information about endangered animals and plants from the U.S. Fish and Wildlife Service, the organization in charge of 94 million acres of wildlife refuges

http://www.endangeredspecie.com Information, links, books, and publications about rare and endangered species. Also includes information about conservation efforts and organizations

*http://*www.ewt.org.za Endangered South African wildlife

http://forests.org/ Includes forest conservation answers to queries

http://www.iucn.org Details of species, IUCN listings, and IUCN publications. Link to online Red Lists of threatened species at: www.iucnredlist.org

http://www.open.ac.uk/daptf/ DAPTF-Declining Amphibian Population Task Force. Provides information and data about amphibian declines

http://www.panda.org World Wide Fund for Nature (WWF). Newsroom, press releases, government reports, campaigns.

http://www.pbs.org/journeytoamazonia The Amazonian rain forest and its unrivaled biodiversity

www.seaturtlespacecoast.org/ Website of the Sea Turtle Preservation Society

www.traffic.org/turtles Freshwater turtles

INDEX

Words and page numbers in **bold type** indicate main references to the various topics.